JOSEPH ROGGENDORF
BETWEEN DIFFERENT CULTURES

Joseph Roggendorf, S.J.

Foreword

HUGH CORTAZZI

———————————— oOo ————————————

There are not many people who can be said to have built real bridges between cultures and properly understood both European and Japanese cultures. Fr Joseph Roggendorf, S.J., whose memoirs are reproduced here, was surely one of the very few to do so.

Joseph Roggendorf who was the son of an engineer was born in the Rhineland in 1908 as the eldest of eight children. His was a traditional Catholic family and his parents were devout but it was not assumed that Joseph would automatically enter the priesthood. He had only just begun elementary school when the First World War began. The 'senseless cruelty of war' was brought home to him in 1916 by hunger and cold. His father who was a friend of Konrad Adenauer, the future Chancellor of West Germany after the Second World War, believed in one Europe rather than warring states. His son, Joseph, for his part was always a firm advocate of reconciliation and tolerance. Throughout his life he abhorred totalitarianism whether of the extreme right or the extreme left.

At school Joseph studied hard. 'The only single thing' he disliked was 'boredom'. He admits that later when he came to teach in Japan his patience was tried by the slow-learner.

With his parents' encouragement the young Joseph went on

to German secondary school the 'Gymnasium' (the English 'grammar' school equivalent) where his abilities were encouraged and tested. Rather than go to university, however, he opted for the religious life and chose the most demanding of all disciplines – that of the Jesuits.

In his memoir Father Roggendorf recounts that his earliest dreams were all connected with his interest in foreign languages and cultures. The Jesuits recognized his linguistic talents and encouraged his study of literature. He was sent first to France and later to England and Japan. His account of his studies in France and England in the inter-war years shows that his natural sense of curiosity and intuitive human understanding stood him in good stead.

The first Japanese whom he got to know had the qualities which Father Roggendorf most respected in his Japanese friends. These were 'warm-heartedness, a capacity for listening, discernment in human relations, and politeness'. He reached Japan for the first time in 1935 and his entire energy was consumed by learning Japanese. It was decided by his superiors that he should return to England to study at London University so that he could work in the English literature department, which had just been established at the Jesuit College in Tokyo, 'Sophia University'. In London, in addition to studying English literature at University College, he enrolled in the Japanese department of the School of Oriental and African Studies as its first graduate student.

Although he was a German national he was able to complete his studies at the university, and having, with difficulty, managed to obtain an exit visa he left England on 21 June 1940 – only a few days after the pitiful evacuation of the British forces at Dunkirk. He then experienced many hardships during the war years in Japan. He recounts these experiences with restraint and sympathetic understanding.

Father Roggendorf soon became a significant figure in the growing Jesuit university where his wide knowledge of Japanese and European culture brought him great respect. He was almost equally knowledgeable about English, German, French and Japanese literature. His interests were wide and he could discuss eruditely almost any topic in the fields of politics, philosophy and ethics as well as literature. He was universally respected as a teacher.

His memoir was written for a Japanese readership. As a result, although it assumes some knowledge of Japan, its insights into Japan and the Japanese character are sensitive. His understanding of German, English and French cultures enables him to make interesting analogies.

As a committed Christian, it seems to me that Father Roggendorf pursued the path to true humility. This, perhaps unfortunately for the reader, who did not know him, means that he is very reticent about his own actions and achievements. Professor Edward Seidensticker's Introduction certainly helps to rectify this and gives the reader some fascinating insights into Father Roggendorf's character, as well as his own.

I did not know Father Roggendorf as well as Professor Seidensticker did, but I recall vividly his personality and his contributions to an informal discussion group of which I was a member in the 1960s. The Japanese members included Kiuchi Nobutane, economist, Fukushima Shintaro, president of Kyodo News Agency and *The Japan Times*, Kano Hisaakira, head of the Yokohama Specie Bank in London before the war and briefly governor of Chiba prefecture, and Wakaizumi Kei, political philosopher. We also had American, German and French members as well as the head of the Chinese Nationalist news agency in Tokyo, all of whom were interested in the economic and political development of Japan, which were the main topics we discussed. After I returned to Japan as British Ambassador in 1980 I was glad to greet Father Roggendorf again as an old friend, but I did not have the time to try to re-establish our old discussion group and did not see so much of him as I had in earlier times. I was saddened by his untimely death and mourned with his many friends and colleagues at the memorial mass for him at the Jesuit Church in Sophia University.

I had not then realized that he had written a memoir which was published in Japanese by the prestigious publishing house Bungei Shunjū in 1983 shortly after his death. Indeed, I only learnt of the existence of the English typescript of this memoir in 2002, when an old friend who had worked for Sir Francis Rundall, one of my predecessors as British Ambassador to Japan, Primrose Croy (née Winch) asked me whether, knowing of my respect for Father Roggendorf, as well as my interest in Japanese affairs generally, I would be interested to see it. It had been given to Primrose by Father Roggendorf's secretary about whom Edward Seidensticker writes so warmly in his Introduction. I immediately responded positively. When I began to read it I thought that it could well be of interest to a wider readership – both for the opportunity to explore the remarkable personality of its author and for the narrative itself detailing his upbringing and early years, but especially his experiences in and attitude to his 'second country' Japan and his relationship with the Japanese people They would also, I thought, be fascinated by the way in which he had built bridges between such different cultures and by his ability to understand cultural differences. Paul Norbury of Global Oriental to whom I sent the typescript shared my impression of the memoir and Professor Seidensticker gladly contributed the Introduction which helps to portray the personality behind the memoir.

I should add that I am not a Catholic, but I share Father Roggendorf's interest in European and Japanese cultures, and his hatred of totalitarianism.

He was very European and, although there was no trace of the *Junker* in him, he was very German and very proud of it. I thought of him as an Old World gentleman. Whatever the dictionary definitions, Old World means for most Americans Western Europe. He was proud of being from an old part, a Catholic part and an anti-Nazi part of Germany. He liked to say that only a German could be completely, utterly, thoroughly anti-Nazi. He liked to point out that the line between Protestant and Catholic Germany follows roughly the frontier of the Roman Empire. I had no trouble understanding why this fact should be so important to him. I did not doubt that it was a fact. I never looked into it. I assumed he knew what he was talking about. He liked to say that Sophia lived off Frings benefits. This was a reference to the cardinal archbishop of Cologne, who was very generous in his gifts to the university.

Already a Jesuit, he was studying in England when the Second World War began. It was his second stay in England, the first having preceded his first time in Japan. He did not want to go back to Germany He wanted to go to Japan. He often spoke of how kind the British authorities were in seeing him on his way. He said that they allowed him to take far more books with him than the regulations permitted. It is hard to see why there should have been limits on the number of books an enemy alien was allowed to take out of the country. Just possibly the story was a tiny white lie. It does not seem to me to matter much. That he should have told it, and repeatedly, was evidence of a lasting and much-deserved gratitude. If he had been in Germany he would probably have had to flee in the night.

There is a kind of European for whom 'Anglo', referring to the English-speaking world, is an expression of distaste. He was not one of them. He was fond of America and Americans and American culture. I may say that this much endeared him to me. He liked American speech and he liked American humour. He was very fond of the earthy American expression 'to get caught with his pants down' and was always seeking devices for getting it into a conversation. He was especially fond of Jewish-American humour, surely one of the richest elements. From him I had a Jewish story, too long to repeat here, and very funny, of how Jesus got his name.

Although his own graduate studies were in England and he was fond of England he did not insist that his disciples go there. If they preferred America to England they went. It was for this reason that I was honoured to have among my students at the University of Michigan the gentleman who is now president of Sophia.

I am not quite sure what the expression 'Jesuitic' means. Not very pleasant connotations of craftiness and cunning seem inescapable. My readings in Chinese history, not a subject in which I have specialized, persuade me that, with regard to the Rites Controversy of late imperial China, it indicates a willingness to compromise. The Jesuits were willing to compromise on what seemed to them secondary matters that they might concentrate on primary ones.

If this is a proper use of the word, then Father Roggendorf was Jesuitic. He was not an obsessive proselytizer. He seemed to think that many a case could be left to its own devices. He seems to have thought that in my case. I was reared a Catholic and go on being one, but we very rarely talked about religion. Perhaps he thought that if I needed help I would tell him, and in the meantime I could get on quite well without him. And perhaps he thought me irrelevant to his main mission, the conversion of the Japanese.

He did not disdain an occasional wry remark about a fellow Jesuit. Of one of them he said: 'He may look like St Aloysius but he gets what he wants.' That he should have said it to an outsider told me that whatever else 'Jesuitic' might mean it did not mean closed and clannish.

At no time, in any event, did he seem holier than the Pope. I once said to him that I thought sex very clearly a thing of

Caesar's, and that the church ought to render it unto that person. Certainly that would make the church easier to live with. He smiled and reminded me that matrimony is a sacrament, and said nothing further. I think possibly he agreed with me.

I do not know where he would be placed in the political spectrum of the Jesuits, but would describe him as a liberal in an early sense, indicating tolerance and broad-mindedness. We never had anything that could remotely be called a heated discussion of politics, but sometimes I was to the left of him and sometimes I was to the right of him. It was not he who changed. It was I. I wobbled. He was steadfast.

I would not say that we got on poorly when I first met him, over a half century ago. We did not get on swimmingly, exactly, either. Though I did not cease being a Catholic, there was a time when I was suspicious of the clergy. The years shortly after the Second World War were such a time. I am ashamed to say that I went on too long thinking of Stalin and the Soviet Union as allies.

When I awakened to my youthful insanity I swung rather far to the right. I was outraged at the simplistic way in which the most vociferous of Japanese intellectuals viewed the world. They saw it in black and white. Black was something known as capitalism, whose headquarters were in Washington, or possibly New York. White was something called socialism and its capital was Moscow (Peking did not seem to matter hugely in those years). Father Roggendorf was thus to be found on my left. He had not changed at all. This state of affairs persisted roughly through my first decade in Tokyo, which ended in 1958. Father Roggendorf and I generally agreed in political matters thereafter. This is to say, essentially, that I came to see that he had been right all along.

Probably the most famous incident in which we were comrades in intellectual and moral arms is what is known as the Koestler Incident of 1959. The origins of this were in the awarding of the Nobel Prize to Boris Pasternak in 1958. The Koestler

Incident was earlier known as the Incident of the Three Foreigners. Outraged by the willingness of the Japanese PEN to condone the behaviour of the Soviet government, three of us sent a protest to the press. The three were Father Roggendorf, Ivan Morris, a scholar of Japanese literature who was born with both British and American citizenship and chose British, and myself. Walking together to another appointment after a PEN meeting, Morris and I decided that something must be done. I said that it would be good to have a non-Anglo with us, and suggested Father Roggendorf. I was sure that he would agree. He may have preferred to stay away from politics, but this was a matter of morals.

We attracted more attention in the papers than I had expected, and then came Koestler. He came visiting early in 1959, and joined in our disapproval of the PEN. The incident promptly became his and not ours. I have no complaints. He was a person of international fame and we were not, and because of him the incident came to the attention of everyone in the land who read a newspaper.

The incident did not have immediate consequences. The PEN did not change its position, essentially a pro-Soviet one. It was not long afterwards, however, that the venomous secretary and office manager of the PEN was dismissed by the president, the novelist and Nobel laureate Kawabata Yasunari. She had been the leader of the pro-Soviet 'liberals' at the PEN, and after her departure it was different. Her name, like that of Father Roggendorf's secretary, was Matsumoto. Koestler got the credit, but I think Father Roggendorf better deserved it.

The other Matsumoto, dear person, has waited long enough for some attention. She was a devout Catholic and nun-like in her dedication. She was even nun-like in her appearance. I sometimes wondered why she did not become a nun. Perhaps the answer is that if she had been in a nunnery she could not have dedicated herself to the good father's service. She was with him through most of his career at Sophia.

Something like a third of a century ago a big newspaper ran a series of articles in which men wrote about women, not their wives, whom they admired. Invited to contribute, I proposed to write about Otama. When I told her so she indicated horror. She did not fit, she said. In a way she was right. The title of the series was *Suteki na Onna*, which might be rendered 'Gorgeous Creatures'. As I have already suggested, Otama was a rather plain woman, and she dressed rather drably. I argued that women could be gorgeous in respects other than physical, and got her to go and be photographed looking down over the outer moat of the castle, where Sophia reposes. The article appeared, and people, if they were telling the truth, liked it; and I think Otama was pleased.

She died last year. I was in Honolulu when a cousin of hers, also a friend of mine, called to give me the news. I immediately called Michael Cooper, a former Jesuit who lives in Honolulu, and asked whether he had heard it. We both called Sophia, which had not. A result was that a large number of Jesuits attended her funeral, among them my former student, the president of the university. I was pleased and grateful. I am sure that Otama, watching from somewhere, it could only be heaven, was too.

CHAPTER ONE

Childhood and Youth

——————————— oOo ———————————

Iwas born in 1908, the eldest of eight children. My father was an engineer, as his father had been, production manager of a railway carriage factory, while my mother's father had been an architect. Both hailed from Mechernich, a town of some 10,000 inhabitants west of Cologne. The name of the town is probably the germanized form of the Latin 'Macriniacum', itself the romanized form of some Celtic name, perhaps a soldier who had settled here on a plot of land received upon retiring from the Roman legion. Relics of the Celtic as well as the Roman past abound in the vicinity. Mechernich lies on the slope of the hilly region called the Eifel. (The Paris Eiffel Tower was erected by an engineer named Gustave Eiffel whose parents had emigrated from a town not far from mine and had adopted the name of the Eifel mountains from where they hailed.) Here the Romans collected the water which, by grandiose aqueducts, made of stone and bricks, were brought all the way to Colonia Agrippina, predecessor of modern Cologne (Köln).

The relics of the past – from Druid shrines, to Roman roads, and arches, and early Germanic cottages became the object of my father's passionate interest. His hobby was *Heimatgeschichte* (local history). He wrote articles and books about the history of our region, but he also worked actively for the preservation of monuments. The 'old' church on top of the hill dominating the town is a memorial to his name – more so than the street named after him. The church, which was abandoned when a new one in the centre of town was erected in the middle of the nineteenth century, had been built on the site of a Roman fort; indeed, the massive spire partly consisted of the old fortress tower. Owing to my father's initiative, the church was restored and put to use again during the 'twenties. In its old cemetery he now lies buried and there, next to him, I interred my mother when she died in 1974, at the age of ninety-six. Their names are engraved on a piece of polished silt from a Roman aqueduct.

As I stood there some time ago looking down on my native town and, further to the east, the plain of Cologne, I felt that it was here, at this spot, that my interest in the intermingling of cultures had begun. The church itself in its present early romanesque style goes back to the tenth century; it is contemporary, therefore, to Ariwara no Narihira's *Ise Monogatari*[1] (Tales of Ise – a collection of brief, lyrical episodes with poems) on which I wrote my *gakui rombun* (degree essay) at London University. Its foundation as well as most of its stones may go back another thousand years. To the South-West, the Seven Mountains (Siebengebirge) can be seen, scene of the old Germanic Siegfried saga and of Wagner's *Nibelungen-Ring*, as well as the two mighty spires of Kölner Dom (Cologne Cathedral). The plain is strewn with towns and villages, clustering around ancient churches. It is criss-crossed by roads, most of the haphazard type to connect cottages and fields; some, however, solid and straight, stone-paved by Caesar, tree-lined by Napoleon, widened, with bridges and tunnels by Hitler: all planned by dictators to transport troops.

As I recently stood again in front of the local war memorial beneath the church on the hill with the names of hundreds of our and our fathers' classmates and relatives, my own memories of World War I welled up. It was in August 1914. That April, at the age of six, I had entered elementary school. Troop trains were rolling through our town, filled with cheerful young soldiers waving and waved at. The graffiti they had chalked on the outside of the trains boasted of quick victory, of early glorious return to the fatherland etc. And I could read them and report them home at lunch as I came back from school. School life must be more difficult for the Japanese child today. The writing of adults – the *kanji* (characters) in Japan – cannot be mastered as easily as our twenty-six alphabetical letters.

It took only a few weeks for me to feel, for the first time, that war was not all cheers and smiles. My favourite teacher, Mr Türk, had been mobilized in the early days and soon news came that he had fallen. I was shaken with sobs as I told my parents. He had been good to me. My mother later used to tell the story that I had come home, one day in the early weeks of that spring, and I said: 'Mama, Teacher Türk has patted me on the head and said he was proud of me.' He died on the blood-drenched fields of Flanders, with tens of thousands of bright-eyed youngsters from three European countries.

Like him, they all believed in the justice of their respective causes. Much later I came across a poem which Charles Péguy[2] had written around that time:

> *Heureux ceux qui sont morts*
> *Dans une guerre juste*
>> (Blessed are those who died in a
>> war fought for justice)

Péguy, of course, thought that justice was on the side of his country. It would have been blasphemy for this naïve patriot to admit even an element of justice on the German side. Yet, even those Germans like my father and my uncles (one of whom was killed), while not happy to have to fight for detested Prussia, were yet sure they were fighting for an unjustly encircled Germany.

All this was far from my child's mind. One thing, however, brought home to me the senseless cruelty of war – although I would have been unable to formulate such thoughts – hunger and cold. From 1916 on, the effects of the British-enforced blockade came to be felt all over Europe. The daily fare was turnips – of the kind fed to cattle – one little piece of meat a week, bread made from wheat mixed with ground beech and oak leaves, and what little we might smuggle in from the country. This lasted for us on the left bank of the Rhine until the war's end, but for most of Germany beyond the Rhine the blockade continued until the Peace Treaty of Versailles was signed in 1919. Resentment at seeing the old, the women and the children becoming the target of military action was one of the reasons for the rising chauvinism in later years in Germany.

Soon, in November 1918 (in Japan it was the time of *Kome Sōdō* (the rice riots) our troops passed again through our town, hollow-eyed, emaciated, in rags – like the musketeers in Remarque's[3] *Im Westen nichts Neues* (Nothing New on the Western Front) – came through on trains, in horse-drawn carriages, on trucks, on foot. As soon as they disappeared across the Rhine, there followed the Allied soldiery. First, we had Scots who would teach us their football tricks and generally fraternize with the children. Then the French. They kept away from us and we from them. On both sides, some shyness was involved, no doubt. The language of the French, let alone their eating and dressing habits, the way of the men kissing each other on both cheeks, were so totally different from ours, that we felt like complete strangers. Certainly, with us easy-going, open-hearted Rhinelanders no enmity was involved. Or was my family the exception? It is true that my mother was so deep a believer, she could not stand others being denounced as enemies since for her they were, literally, brothers, namely children of the same father in heaven. And my father thought, even then, in terms of one Europe rather than warring states. He was a federalist, very much like Konrad Adenauer, a good acquaintance of his, and, like Adenauer, he was later unjustly accused of being a separatist (secessionist), i.e., advocating political autonomy for the Rhineland, while he really only wanted the limited regional autonomy, which we now have in the Federal Republic of Germany. His thinking was so deeply rooted in history that he resented the unification of Germany under upstart Prussia at the price of excluding Austria.

Such things I might have overheard occasionally in adult conversation. In those days I was interested in school and my classmates. I dare say, I was an enthusiastic schoolboy. The only single thing I remember disliking in elementary school and Gymnasium (middle, high) was boredom. That usually set in when a teacher felt it necessary to explain the same thing again and again until the last slow-mover had understood. Later, in the classroom in Japan, where as a foreigner I always had to do some language teaching, what tested my patience most was the slow-learner or rather the student who, all of a sudden, becomes doggedly silent, instead of stating what it is that he does not understand. That the Japanese keep silent in certain circumstances, I have come much later to appreciate as valuable wisdom, and patience is the only wisdom increasing with my age. I hope I am forgiven by my former students for the irritability of earlier years.

But to revert to my school days. As the war went on, my parents decided, instead of letting me commute by train to the Gymnasium fifteen kilometres away, to keep me at home while the war continued. I would attend elementary school for a year or two more. So as to enable me to enter a higher class of Gymnasium, they arranged for tutorials in Latin. I was then eight years old. Upon the prompting of my mother – who had something of the unjustly maligned *Kyōiku Mama* (education-obsessed mother) of Japan about her – our assistant parish priest, Fr Mause, set up a private school (*juku*) for five boys of about my age. We were to meet in his house twice a week. I bought my copy of Ostermann-Müller's Latin Primer and, for the first time in my life, plunged into the ocean of a foreign language. I remember reverently taking the book home and peering at the last page giving examples of Latin proverbs with the German translation. *Gutta cavat lapidem/Steter Tropfen höhlt den Stein.* (A steady drop hollows the stone). Erroneously I connected the German rather rare adjective *steter* (equivalent to the English 'steady') to the Latin, thinking it meant 'stone'. But this initial mistake I shamefully kept to myself.

That the Latin lessons went smoothly was largely due to the personality of Fr Mause. A graduate from Bonn University, he was not only an admirable pastor, a capable musician (every year he directed one large Oratorio with local talent only, my father being a valued tenor), but also a model pedagogue. Later, I often thought he would have been a greater success in Japan as a teacher than I ever was. He never raised his voice, was imperturbably friendly, always encouraged and never reprimanded. He radiated goodness, and at morning Mass – where we boys would serve at the altar in turn – his devotion impressed itself on our young minds. Maybe without my being aware of it, the thought of one day becoming a priest began to stir in me at that time.

Still, as I reflect now, I would have learned Latin regardless of who my teacher was. I had an interest in language as such, as people began to notice. An uncle once remarked how easily I could switch from pure dialect to pure high German. Most dialect-speakers fall into the trap of either pronouncing the standard language with a heavy local accent, or else apply standard language patterns to the dialect. In addition, I had a specially burning interest in Latin as such. After all, it was the language of our first civilizers, the Romans. And it was also the language of Mass in the morning and of compline on Sunday evening.

In March 1919, a few months after the armistice, Fr Mause had us try the admittance examination for the third class of

Gymnasium. We had just completed five years of elementary school, and the usual thing would have been to complete four years and enter the first class of Gymnasium. We were told to aim two classes higher. Well, when the dust settled, I alone had succeeded. The other four dropped one or two classes below.

I have since witnessed the anguish of entrance examinations in the highly competitive society of Japan. The atmosphere of one's family is probably most important. An intelligent level of table talk, an interest in books, an equal interest in games and sports, and a relaxed, cheerful air – these are remedies against examino-phobia. Anxious as my mother was to see me succeed, she never made me feel that either her or my own happiness depended on the success or failure of an examination.

My Gymnasium days from 1919 to 1926 coincided with a very dark era of modern German history. But to me they were days of unmitigated delight. I was the youngest in the class, having jumped one year, and my nickname became 'Röggelchen' which means 'little rye bread' (*Roggen* in my name is etymologically the same as rye in English); *Röggelchen* are the little brown buns made of rye flour, a favourite breakfast dish in the Rhineland. The general air was of such carelessness and euphoria as, certainly in the last one or two years of the new-style high schools (*Shinsei Kōtō gakkō*), it is not so easy to encounter in Japan. Ours was a good average school, not a particularly distinguished school (*meimon gakkō*). One went to the nearest available school, and that was usually good enough. It is true that the percentage of children of the same year to enter secondary schools was then infinitely smaller than now; hence it was usually a talented minority. But in any case, less is expected at school from the average youngster at an ordinary German school than from the young Japanese here. To learn the *kanji* (Chinese characters) system plus two syllabaries and, in addition, *rōmaji* (roman letters), is not comparable to acquiring twenty-six letters, especially since the German vocabulary (as also the French and English) is half of the Japanese.

16

When it comes to learning English for a Japanese boy of twelve, the difficulties must be frightful. I doubt if, as a youngster, I had been confronted with, say, Japanese, I would have caught fire as I did with Latin. No doubt, it is a good thing that English has become the world language; it has hardly any changing word endings, no genders in nouns, and few irregular nouns or verbs. So it is deceptively easy in the beginning. But, with its absence of rules for grammar and pronunciation, it gets increasingly difficult. To write a letter, let alone an essay, idiomatically and correctly, is almost impossible for a nonnative English speaker; indeed, for few native English speakers. Yet hundreds of thousands of young Japanese set out anew each year to conquer this frighteningly alien world. They also learn more about the history and geography, the music, literature and philosophy of the West than we ever acquire about the East. And then consider the height of mathematical skill they achieve! The dedication of so many parents and teachers, and the indomitable vigour of so many youths, are indeed the glory of Japan. I find nothing harder to forgive than the arrogance of foreigners belittling Japanese intelligence or education merely because of the broken English they speak.

If it were not for their already crowded curriculum, Latin would be a brilliant instrument to sharpen the mind of gifted Japanese youngsters. No doubt, I owe to the study of Latin an immense widening of the verbal horizon, of historical perspectives, and a new way to literature. Latin has stayed with me. I still read it with ease and pleasure. But I am afraid that I cannot say the same of Greek which, in those days, was started in the fourth grade of gymnasium to be continued for six years until graduation. Greek is a noble, subtle language, but in the teaching of it, too much time was lost in trying to master the details of a complicated grammar and memorize words and phrases that were never to occur again in later life. I understand that at present the teaching of Greek, where it is still taught at all, is being much simplified and, in effect, reduced to teaching only the vocabulary which has entered modern philosophy, aesthetics, medicine and science.

Maybe there are Japanese who compare the time and energy given to English in middle-high schools with the actual use of English in adult life and conclude that it is useless. Still, I am inclined to think that the learning of English in Japan should never be considered a waste of time, (as I am now inclined to think Greek was for us). Studying English is the best way of obtaining, however vague, a knowledge of thinking processes outside the small, sealed-off, island-world of Japan. I am glad to see the habit growing among my friends and students of reading some English at home or when commuting. Not everybody has the musical ear and the gift of mimicry, let alone the opportunity, to learn to *speak*. But everybody can get hold of newspapers, magazines and paperbacks in English and learn to commune with the world beyond the confines of these islands of Japan. In fact, to do so is an indispensable condition for internationality.

Modern languages were treated with less seriousness in the classical or *humanistisch* Gymnasium of those days. (Of course, two other types of Gymnasium existed, both available in the town; one with emphasis on modern languages and less Latin, one with emphasis on mathematics, science and one modern language.) Major subjects of the classical Gymnasium were: German, mathematics, Latin and Greek. All the other subjects were minor, including history, art, science and modern languages. French was started in the third grade, i.e., the year I enrolled. The teacher, a swarthy, bespectacled little gentleman pronounced French nasals in his high-pitched voice in a manner which we considered somewhat affected. He also made exaggerated 'French' gestures and even wore – horrible thought to the Germanic mind – a discreet perfume. As a matter of fact, he managed to lay solid foundations, as I later discovered when going to France on hiking tours and, later still, for a spell of study.

Unfortunately, the study of French was suddenly disrupted.

In 1923, in the middle of the inter-war peace, the French Army occupied Germany's industrial centre, the Ruhr District. The object was to extract and transport the coal which the Germans were not paying quickly enough by way of reparations. It was a clumsy action on the part of the French government and the German reaction – passive resistance – was equally ill-inspired, namely total refusal to cooperate. For us schoolboys one of the regrettable consequences was the abolition of French from the curriculum.

Instead of French, English was introduced. We studied English during the three years until graduation. I am sorry to have to confess that none of us took it very seriously. The language struck us as altogether too easy – indeed, almost like a German dialect. But our attitude was to a great extent the fault of our professor, a highly learned scholar in the field of Turco-Altaic languages which he taught at Cologne University, very absent-minded, and of a trusting nature. He would not notice our cheating, and so we cheated.

I still remember Dr L. sitting on the rostrum ensconced behind a newspaper, never once looking up. We were supposed to write our written examination. In fact, two of us were doing the work, my friend G. handling the grammar, I handling the dictionary. We wrote answers, which were then passed from desk to desk. A professor, passionately interested in odd European languages such as Finnish or Hungarian, allegedly of Ural-Altaic background, must have considered English an easy game, not to be taken too seriously. I met him again, some thirty years later. I had been in Japan for two decades and he was burning to find out all about Japanese, especially whether the kinship of Japanese with Hungarian, or Finnish, or perhaps Basque, was still admitted by scholars. And did Japanese, as an agglutinative language, have advantages over our 'flexive' languages? I had to speak a few sentences and, although eighty and very hard of hearing, he managed to catch what I said. Did I think he might still learn it, he asked me anxiously. He showed me the Bible in Japanese in his possession, a Meiji (1868–1912) edition if I remember correctly.

Speaking of teachers revisited, I managed to see one more that same year – Prof. H., one of my two mathematics professors. I was surprised that he remembered me and thought well of me, although I never was a mathematical genius. He knew in Japan that the standard of mathematics was high in schools and wanted me to explain the reasons. All I could think of was to mention the proverbial dedication (*kimben*) and *Gründlichkeit* (thoroughness) (*tetteisa*). He listened attentively to the examples I narrated of Japanese attitudes to work and to their devotion and loyalty. He then remarked:

> These are qualities which will ensure their future. The young generation in Germany is losing some of that. We have wrought an 'economic miracle'. And already we sit back to enjoy it rather than working at it. I'm afraid Hitler has deeply damaged the soul of the German nation.

One of my teachers I would have liked to hear on the same subject – namely the state of the German nation, as compared with Japan – was no longer alive. Prof. P. had been my most inspiring and most efficient teacher in classical languages. He was a student of Wilamowitz-Möllendorf, of Berlin University, one of the two or three greatest Hellenists of this century. From that great man in Berlin, P. *Sensei* had not only learned his classical languages but also some of his political views. Although a Rhinelander himself, he proclaimed the views of the typical Prussian *Junker*: contempt of the Weimar Republic, of Austria, of the Jews, in short – and I was too young to see it then – many of the destructive Hitler ideas of a later time. Happily, I was totally impervious to such ideas, thanks to my religious training and my paternal heritage of ideas. But apart from his ideological prejudices, P. had a gift for making youngsters like myself love to grapple with languages and pierce through to the beauty of another country's literature. I still remember glowing with happiness when, one day, he returned a written translation from the

Greek with the exclamation: 'Roggendorf, I gave you an A+; and here is the reason' ... In the great story of the Spartan mother whose son has been killed in the war, she said, when commiserated with: 'I knew I had born a mortal being' and instead of the verb 'to bear (*umu*)' – no longer used in modern German – I had used the expression 'be the mother of'.

Only a few of my old teachers were still alive when I returned to Germany for the first time after twenty-one years in Japan. One of these few I refused to look up. Perhaps it was the wrong thing to do. But I could not face seeing old Prof. H. again who had taught us religion, one hour a week, for some five years. He was a learned man with a doctorate in church art. He was also well prepared for his classes. But there was nothing to attract the young heart to the kind of Christianity he would expound in the classroom, and there was little problem consciousness in his treatment of moral matters. He had also an almost morbid attitude of *suki-kirai* (like-dislike) – acknowledging some of the pupils and ignoring others. Now that I have grown old, I am inclined to think of him with more sympathy. One-sidedness is a frequent failure of educators, and in his case, it was accentuated by shyness. Furthermore, religion is definitely one of the hardest subject-matters to teach. In the German public school system it was a part of the curriculum, and the idea is not only to *teach* about religion but to expound its significance in the value system. (This was abolished by the Nazis and partly reinstalled after the war.)

A few years ago, I had an experience in Tokyo connected with this topic. At a reception, a member of the Soviet Embassy, upon recognizing me as a priest, began to discuss religion. 'I have absolutely no feeling for religion, since it is not taught in our schools,' he said. I explained that, from my experience, most people do not believe because they are taught at school. The influence of the family, the cultural atmosphere, the example of friends goes much deeper. He looked at me rather incredulously. My answer had apparently upset what he had memorized from Soviet textbooks. As can happen, the unbeliever may be less tolerant than the believer. He would have been totally at a loss to explain how I could have so heartily disliked my religious instructor, a priest, at school and yet become a man of religion (*shūkyōka*) myself.

The last examination was a solemn affair. Our teachers prepared three sets of questions for the written examination. These were submitted to the Commissioner for Education in the various provinces, in my case the Rhineland. He selected one of the three sets, and this set was unsealed in the principal's office on the day of our written examination. Several days after the examination, the oral was held in the presence of the Commissioner or one of his deputies.

As we were waiting to be called in for the oral, a teacher arrived to announce that three of us had been exempted from the oral because of high achievement including in the written examination. I was one of them. This was a highly desirable honour, but I had not been sure whether I would qualify, since because of a change of teachers, I had had some difficulties in mathematics. My parents were proud of me, and my mother said: 'I knew it would happen.'

I look back with happiness on my Gymnasium days. They were pervaded by a feeling of cheerfulness and trust. There was quite a bit of sternness, too. Quite a few of my comrades were failed at the start of the final two years: this was called *Majorsecke*, i.e., the point where, in the Army, a captain could be made a major, and if this did not happen, he might not be able to proceed to the rank of colonel or general. But one's destiny was decided by one's own trusted teachers. So also the final, big examination. This opened the way to any university in the country.

Alas, things in Germany have not remained what they were in my time, fifty years ago. The hankering for college education, so characteristic of egalitarian industrial societies, has deeply affected Germany too. Indeed, in Japan the new trend has been understood much earlier than in Europe. From the end of the war onwards, colleges here have been allowed to multiply. Around 40% of the respective age group can now enter a university in Japan. This is a good thing. But it must also be admitted that, in the name of equality of opportunity, a glaring inequality of actual choice has also resulted. Some schools are more desirable, hence more difficult to enter, than others. Sons and daughters of the upper level of society are thus favoured, while others are discriminated against. Still, the Japanese have created college facilities for more than two million students – *Tandai* (short-course universities) included – while in Germany there is now, after the efforts of the last ten or fifteen years, barely room for 870,000 in sixty universities. The most praiseworthy thing about Japanese higher education is that so many parents finance it themselves with dedication and zeal: parents directly support private colleges (91% private junior, 74% of other colleges). In Europe, the state is more generous in paying, but parents are requested to contribute less.

My schoolboy days coincided with the post-First World War period when, in anarchist confusion, the Weimar Republic was painfully being established, while beneath the surface of a model democratic constitution a totalitarian movement already began to stir. Dissatisfaction with the unjust clauses of the Versailles Treaty of 1919 was what every German, regardless of his party politics, agreed upon. But my classmates as well as their parents disapproved of radical solutions, in the way Rhinelanders have, namely by laughing about passionately-propounded extremes. Figures of the ultra-left as well as the ultra-right were annually made fun of in the carnival parades in Rhineland towns. There were only two exceptions to political moderation I can think of while at school.

A Gymnasium classmate Karl T., son of a local Elementary School principal, was not a bad pupil, but somewhat reserved and with very few friends. One morning he did not turn up. He had been particularly taciturn of late and rushed away as soon as class was over. Soon rumours leaked out that he had been with a group of right-wing terrorists and had helped to blow up, in those days of the French occupation of the Ruhr in 1923, a railway bridge not far away. There were mysterious comings and goings by police. Karl T. never returned to school. He must have left for the other side of the Rhine where the occupation army had no power.

The other case concerns P. *sensei*: mentioned above. His vulgar remarks against Jews – we had one Jewish boy in our class – which he would make at any opportunity, sounded all the more repulsive as they came from so educated a man. At any rate, he had no influence on us whatsoever, and I think he knew it. He was transferred to another town.

Rhinelanders are not easily turned into fanatics. A humorous story is told about the Rhinelanders' characteristic unconcern with ideological narrowness. The Rhineland had been made into a province of Prussia (Preussen) at the time of the Congress of Vienna. This had been initiated by the English, grateful for Prussian help at Waterloo, that decisive battle against Napoleon. The story goes that a school inspector from Berlin asked in primary school class: 'Now, children, tell me, what is a *Ketzer* (heretic)?' He was convinced that in this Catholic province it was a matter of daily routine to speak evil of 'heretic' Protestants. But no one raised a hand.

The children had never heard that word in their lives. Until one little boy finally ventured: 'It is the name for a male cat.' An unwittingly ingenious answer, since *die Katze* is the female cat, the male really is *Kater*, but *Kätzer* sounds plausible enough.

More than by politics, then still rather remote from the daily lives of Gymnasium pupils, we were troubled by economic realities. My classmates all came from middle-class families, and had all become impoverished through the astronomical inflation of those years. Being the eldest of a family of eight, I felt the misery of poverty more than the others. I led a frugal life for many post-war years. I bought all my school books second-hand and sold them again to younger pupils. By way of *Arbeit* (work) I gave tutorials in Latin. And I also received a scholarship at the Gymnasium. I would not have managed without them. Fortunately, there is more justice now for the less privileged.

By 1924, the economy was being restored and by the time of my graduation two years later the family was slowly recovering, my father being in the prime of his life and my mother being a great helpmate to him and cheerful guide to her many children. The inflation, as much as the Versailles Treaty, contributed to demoralizing the German middle class. A proletarian psychology gave birth to the radicalism out of which the totalitarian movements of Left and Right grew.

I suppose if a Japanese is asked to state what he remembers best from his school-days, it will probably be the friends he made; and if questioned further, it may turn out that they were not necessarily all his classmates, but rather the *dōsōkai*, or all those having looked out through the 'same window' of the classroom. Friends for life are probably made in the various circles, clubs, *kenkyūkai* (study groups), *dōkōkai* (groups from the same school) etc. German youngsters at the Gymnasium also like to gather in this manner, although not quite with the enthusiasm and dedication of their Japanese counterparts. Incidentally, I feel impelled here to say a word of encouragement about club activities (*kurabu-katsudō*). No doubt, it can get out of hand, and bad habits of drinking, smoking and games of chance and betting may be contracted that last a lifetime. Nevertheless, in such contexts the virtues of social life (*shakōsei*) can be naturally acquired. And that is an important acquisition in a society stressing *enryo* (reserve), *akirame* (resignation), *hikaeme* (effacement), *fuwaraidō* (blindly following) and thus, while ensuring the avoidance of clashes, which also creates much loneliness. My best friends in the Gymnasium were equally not so much classmates as club members. Although I have spent the greater part of my life abroad –

almost fifty years – I am still in contact with these old friends. But, what is perhaps more important, certain aspects of my personality developed under the influence of the group to which I belonged.

The club I joined – in fact I was one of the founders – belonged to a sub-sector of the youth revival (*shinsei*) movement, known in the modern German history of thought as *Jugendbewegung*. It went back to attempts in the early twentieth century to create a way of life more in keeping with adventure-seeking, nearness to nature and closeness to the people. Much of the style of life can be seen in troops of Boy Scouts or of *Wandervogel*, and much of our activity consisted in undertaking tours on bicycle or on foot, pitching tents, singing old folk songs, and cooking our meals in the open. The national organization of which our circle became a member, was called *Quickborn* (living fountain). Boys from sister groups in nearby towns such as Cologne, Bonn and Aachen came to teach us a few fundamentals. And soon we, too, were seen in our Tolstoy blouses, rucksacks and guitars to astound the stolid burghers. We met once a week near a boat-house on the river, which we had hired, and where we had a self-made canoe or two. During the holidays we swarmed out in groups of three, or even up to ten, for hiking tours, which lasted a few weeks. We established special friendship links with a similar group of French youngsters, met by chance on a trip into the French-speaking Ardennes hills. Occasionally, we were allowed on the large freight ships on the Rhine, travelling up as far as Basel, down as far as Amsterdam and, upon landing, taking to the road.

Our group consisted not only of pupils from our Gymnasium but also of a few from a newly introduced type of higher school, the *Aufbauschule*, for those who after eight years of elementary school – not, as we, after four or five – had decided to enter a shortened higher school to prepare for college. These boys having long wanted to be blue-collar workers were a more down-to-earth type than we. I doubt whether in Japan pupils from high school (*kōkō*) and higher specialist schools (*kōsen*) would mix as easily as we did. At any rate, we got along famously.

The German 'Youth Movement' of the early-twentieth century consisted of numerous organizations, some provincial, some nation-wide. *Quickborn* was religiously orientated. Each group usually had a priest as an adviser. But our own religious enthusiasm was stronger than any adviser could have imparted. We were all for vivifying Church services, offering to sing or to perform a religious drama in church. We would, as we passed a crucifix or a statue of Our Lady erected like a *jizō*[4] (Buddhist statue) by the roadside, stop for a hymn accompanied by flute, violin and guitar.

We were active in social work, too, trying to bring joy and pleasure to orphanages and old folks' homes. One event I remember with particular vividness. At the very height of resentment against the French occupation of the Ruhr, it was decided at our headquarters to start an action of atonement for the wounds inflicted by the German armed forces on French territory during the war. Funds were to be obtained by collecting jewelry to finance German volunteers to rebuild houses and monuments. Some fifty young men were to work in the Marne and Somme districts in the east of France to help the farmers. When I approached my mother and asked if she had any jewelry, she gave me a bitter-sweet smile. 'I have sold all my necklaces, bracelets and broaches to get food for the family,' she said. I was moved to tears. So she had been wearing imitation pieces to spare our feelings. Today, I would call this the samurai spirit. *Bushi wa kuwanedo* ... (the samurai shows no weakness when starving).[5]

Incidentally, the action in the Maine basin took place and was reported to Premier Poincaré in the Chamber of Deputies. His answer, according to the newspaper, was: 'One swallow does not make a summer.'

The highlight of the six years in the movement was for me

my encounter with Fr Romano Guardini, then professor at Berlin University and the spiritual adviser of *Quickborn*. I had read some of his books, one, *Von heiligen Zeichen* (Of holy signs) we had read together in our group. In the summer of 1925, we crossed Germany on foot heading south, in order to attend a study-and-prayer session of several days at Burg Rothenfels in the Spessart Forest, north of Frankfurt over which he presided. This half-ruined castle had been donated to our movement and we had rebuilt it. This *gasshuku* (training camp) was a joyous affair, especially in the evenings round the camp fires. But the climax each day were Father Guardini's appearances, a lecture in the morning and a seminar in the afternoon. He had a quiet, serious, compelling way of speaking, and in the seminar discussions he would listen in the most sympathetic way. What the subjects were which he addressed I have now completely forgotten. But one keenly-felt impression has stayed with me ever since: the joy of religious philosophy and the love of literature are not incompatible with religious faith; they can be both the base and the culmination of faith. Guardini's great books on the dominant figures of the Western tradition have been my constant guideposts in teaching and researching comparative literature: Dante, Pascal, Shakespeare, Dostoevsky and Rilke. Shortly before he died in 1968 he contributed an article to a book I was then editing with a gracious personal note (*Gendai Shichō*, p. 81).

In these first eighteen years of my life, the threads were spun of which the rest of my life's garment was to be woven. In those days the graduation diploma of a German high school was then called *Reife-zeugnis* (Certificate of Maturity). I doubt whether I was in any real sense 'mature'. But I was steadfast enough to begin a journey through a variety of cultures, not only national ones, such as the cultures of France, England and Japan, but also the religion-centred one of a priest and the learning-centred one of a literature professor.

CHAPTER TWO

Entering Religious Life and First Alien Culture Contacts

———————— oOo ————————

I announced my decision to become a priest shortly before I graduated from the Gymnasium, in 1926. The teacher in charge of our class one day inquired, which university twenty of us in the graduating class would choose and what we would study, if we were successful at graduation. My classmates chose law, engineering, literature, medicine, etc.; two, my friend Rick and I, said 'theology'. 'Theology' meant we wanted to be priests. But while Rick specified Bonn as his university where the priests of the diocese of Cologne, our home diocese, were trained, I said: 'I am going to join the Jesuits.' There were some expressions of incredulity, since I was known as lively and enterprising, not like the sedate and rather shy Rick. Rick, who was two or three years older, was the only one I had confided in; in fact, we had done our homework together in the last year or two, he helping me in mathematics and I him in languages.

It was a vital decision. I had talked it over with my father, who at no point discouraged me, but showed a little sadness at the prospect of losing me. Indeed, in contrast to my other friends, including Rick, who chose a university but did not therefore leave home, my decision implied a certain 'loss': farewell to the family on entering a religious house (*shūdōin*). That is what made it so difficult. I found the thought of leaving home harder to bear than the idea that I myself would never have a family to call my own. I must add here, however, that I did not really lose contact with parents and brothers-sisters (*kyōdai*) to the extent I then feared. I could frequently return home and they came to look me up even more often while I was preparing for the priesthood. When I talked to my mother, she was overjoyed. That disappointed me somewhat, since I thought she would miss me most. But, with her deep faith uppermost in her mind, was, no doubt, the thought of being able to return to God a precious gift, her own eldest son, in gratitude for the graces received. The only other person I consulted Fr Geyer, a Jesuit Father in Cologne. I had written clandestinely to my uncle in Japan about my plans to enter the Order. He answered that he could not advise me for or against, since he did not know me and suggested instead his friend in Cologne who then arranged talks with other Fathers. I was allowed to enter the noviciate.

I have often been asked, especially in Japan, why I resolved to be a celibate priest and a member of the Society of Jesus. I can only answer that it came to me as the most natural thing. Certainly there was no *Weltschmerz* (agonizing) involved provided by temperament, unrequited love, disgust with my environment, nor was there the slightest hint of pressure from any side.

I had not always been thinking of the priesthood. I am sure that, like other boys when very young, I must have dreamt of being an engine driver, or a master baker. But my earliest more serious dreams were all connected with my interest in foreign languages and cultures. For a long time I was playing with the idea of being a Gymnasium teacher or perhaps even a university professor. My father reminded me much later of what I had almost forgotten: that I had toyed with the idea of becoming a foreign correspondent. When, finally, I made up my mind, I felt as if an inevitable hand had opened a door for me, the only open door, and had led me onto the path I have trodden ever since.

It is true, a pronounced cultural pessimism was, in the air. Even at school we knew about Spengler's *Untergang des Abendlands.*[6] But given my background and temperament, the thought never entered my mind that the religious house was but a shelter for escapers from a deteriorating world. Rather, perhaps because I had a romantic trait, I thought I might be of use to mankind as a priest rather than in any other capacity. The milieu I had been brought up in was one of harmony of the sacred and the secular, the serious and the hilarious, idealism and practicality. This was very much the case in my home country (*furusato*) in the Rhineland with its sunny, friendly and good-hearted people.

In those days the relationship between man and nature, city and countryside, individual and family had not yet undergone the transformation which the Second Industrial Revolution is now bringing about. The subtle materialism of our present society will pass away one day, we may be sure. But while the hedonism, the pan-sexualism and the consumerism in the rich industrialized countries last, fewer young men and women will find it as easy as it was in my adolescence to find the quiet time to reflect on deeper issues and order one's personal life accordingly.

When, some ten years after having joined the Order, I came to Japan, I was surprised at being constantly asked: 'Why don't you marry?' Even now a taxi-driver will say: 'Your wife must be Japanese, since you speak the language.' When I explain that as a Catholic father (*shimpu*) I am not married, he will usually reply: 'Oh, so you are a *shimpu*. Was your father a *shimpu*, too?'

He does not necessarily suspect that he is, in fact, implying that a priest may not have a wife but perhaps a mistress, in order to have a son. He only sees the church in analogy to the *tera* (temple), or *jinja* (shrine) as bequeathed from father to son. The ideal of the celibate *seishokusha* has almost died out in Japan. Yet Shinran Shōnin's (founder of the Shinshū sect of Buddhism) revolutionary act of taking a wife happened in the Kamakura Period and was for centuries opposed by other sects (*shūha*). Until rather recent history, the idea of an unmarried clergy must have been familiar to many, as it still is in a number of higher religions in East and West alike.

Scepticism or incredulity concerning priestly celibacy has now become much more widespread than forty or fifty years ago. Indeed, there are even within the Church some people advocating its abolition. It is possible to imagine that this may happen, since the institution is definitely not traceable to the biblical revelation itself. Already some Catholic groups, converted from Orthodoxy (*Seikyōkai*), allow married clergy under certain conditions. But as for *shūdōsha* (religious people), and I mean priests leading a common life in *shūdōin* (religious house), in contrast to the parish clergy – I confess that it will either be celibate or not at all. I am sure that the disappearance of all religious orders would leave painful gaps in society as a whole. Throughout the world much of the good work in education, charity and welfare would no longer be done. This would be felt most poignantly in countries of the Third World. I speak from experience; of my four sisters three became nuns, all volunteered for work abroad, one died in India – a woman as great and dedicated as Sister Theresa of Nobel Prize fame, or this is what many people who knew her have told me. Another sister works in Pakistan and a third in Brazil. They were at first engaged in higher education in the countries to which they were assigned to. But they soon turned to the underprivileged and have accomplished heroic deeds, certainly more heroic than anything I have done in Japan. I am glad to be able to report that many Japanese friends of mine are actively support-ing them, and my sister in Brazil writes that the most reliable and understanding of her sisters are *nisei* (second generation) Japanese. In these 'developing' countries people have remained concerned with the essentials of life. Hence the Fathers and Sisters, sharing their life of misery with a smile and the perpet-ual readiness to help, are instinctively trusted, while in our luxury-orientated 'advanced' world indifference prevails.

The Japanese reader will forgive me, I hope, if I keep elabo-rating on the subject of the religious life. It is true that the Japanese as a nation are exceedingly friendly to representatives of religion or, shall I say, at any rate to Christian Fathers and Sisters. People expect wonders from *us*. A mother with a son a drug-addict, or a daughter seduced or attempting suicide nei-ther of them Christians – will come for advice. Once I was stopped near Yotsuya Station by a sobbing girl who absolutely wanted to be a nun, but had not even been baptized. She had been jilted by her boyfriend. She must have considered St Ignatius Church a kind of Kamakura *Tōkeiji*[7] where frustrated women can flee for safety.

But in contrast to this rather romantic evaluation of the reli-gious life, there is also an unsympathetic view. With educated Japanese, it often derives from the books they have read. European literature is full of writers describing the influence of Christianity as oppressively stifling. But the families from which Samuel Butler[8] or George Eliot, Lawrence or Joyce, Hesse or Gide escaped with feelings of relief are not properly Christian families: they are deformed by the predetermination-ist heresy in its various forms, Calvinist, Jansenist, Pietist – a heresy which is indeed bound to lead to hypocrisy, and *dokuzenshugi* (self-righteousness) to phariseeism, the one vice execrated by Christ. Such self-styled representatives of Christianity did exist and, indeed exist still now. Not all priests are saints; indeed, cantankerousness, gaucheness, the tendency to simplify or judge only from abstract principles are a kind of 'professional disease' of many priests. Nevertheless, there is a more basic explanation of the insufficient understanding by modern men, whether in Japan or abroad, of the religious life.

Life in a religious order does constitute a state of cultural polarization. To live apart – in vital points – from the rest of the world, dedicated to the service of God together with like-minded men, is living in a world rather different from that of the salaried man with the joys and worries of his family. The world view of the priest, if he is serious, is centripetal – i.e., God in the centre – that of the non-priest tends to be centrifugal, i.e., preoccupied with the things of this world. Still, it would be against theology as well as common sense to say that one has to be a priest to lead a spiritual life. The world is full of wonderful people who could put a priest to shame. On the other hand, not all priests are living up to their ideals.

I was not worrying so much about issues such as celibacy in those days, since I knew there were ten years till the really irrevocable decision would be made, at ordination. Similarly, I approached the Jesuit Order like a sleep-walker. I was afraid they might not accept me as unworthy of their high standards. As for the accusations against them, I had read enough to conclude that they were untrue. Strictures against the Order can all be traced back to either the religious controversies of the sixteenth century and later centuries or to the expansion of European colonialism, around the same time. In the religious *ronsō* (debate) of those centuries they were accused of 'duplicity' and 'prevarication'. The fact is that they had never held the principle that a good cause sanctifies even a bad means, but only that a good cause sanctifies a means which, in itself, is neither good nor bad. For example fasting as a means for a bad purpose, like unreasonably (*murini*) damaging one s health, would be bad. To fast in order to keep alive and do one's duty would be good. Eating in itself is morally neither good nor bad; it is justified (sanctified) by its ultimate purpose. This alone is implied in the Jesuit slogan 'All for the greater glory of God'.

Their standard does not differ from that of most people, it was only distorted by fanatics in the unfortunate religious controversies of the past.

Pascal,[9] through his vast influence in world literature and thought, is largely responsible for the anti-Jesuit slanders to have entered the history books and encyclopaedias. Pascal's judgement was partially based on forged material delivered into his hand by zealots of Port Royal, the Jansenist brain centre. That certain Fathers used political influence to keep Jansenism from spreading, especially in France, cannot be denied and is to be lamented. But the harm done to mankind wherever the Calvin-inspired doctrine of predestination – according to which only a few are supposed to be saved, the rest is *mass damnata* established itself seems to explain, if not altogether to excuse, the political scheming of certain Paris Jesuits.

It is harder to see, why Pascal should have sided with the enemies of the Order in the matter of acculturation in Japan and China. Valignano,[10] Rodriguez, Frois and other *Kirishitan Paderen* (Christian missionaries) had been overwhelmed by Japanese civilization. But before their efforts to adopt elements from Japanese tradition into the Christian forms of devotion, the persecution began. They would have attracted the anger of the Jansenists as much as did the efforts of Jesuits in China like Ricci[11] and Schall, highly esteemed at the Chinese Imperial Court for their achievements in mathematics and astronomy as well as for their piety, for allowing Christian believers to participate in rites honouring Confucius. It is hard to see a scholar like Pascal failing to appreciate this attempt to break through arrogant Euro-Centrism, and return to the pristine universality of Christianity. Pascal, as a forerunner of existentialist philosophy is, deservedly, highly esteemed in Japan. But the harm done by his and the Jansenists' ethical rigorism is less known, hence his views on the Jesuits are often uncritically accepted. But this is changing with the expanding knowledge of Japanese Western historians. Several years ago I wrote to Nakamura

Yūjirō suggesting a correction in an article by him in *Shisō* (thought) where he had touched on the Jesuits. I also sent him a book I had just then edited, *Yezusu Kai* (published by Enderle Shoten). Prof. Nakamura most obligingly used my note for a lengthy clarification in his masterly book on Pascal.

When I made my way to the Noviciate, more than fifty years ago, doubts about the excellence of the Order were far from my mind. I was proud that they had accepted me and still am. Indeed, I am grateful for two decisions affecting my life which were made by my own free will: to become a Jesuit priest and to have come to Japan. This I have never regretted.

We were about a dozen to enter the first year of noviciate (of which there are now two) and there were about the same number in the second year, mostly fresh from Gymnasium, all from what became West Germany. (There were two more noviciates in Germany, one in the East, one in the South.) Our life was regulated rather austerely. We had fixed times for personal meditation and common prayer, lectures and discussions, meals (during which a book was read aloud), eating and sleeping. We had enough time for tennis and football as well as for walks around the rather monotonous landscape of the lower Rhine. The Father in charge was a well-intentioned, studious and conscientious man, but neither inspiring nor humorous. So we looked forward to the various Fathers passing through occasionally and inspiring us with talks about their particular activities: pastors, teachers, conferenciers, editors or writers.

To one talk I listened with especially rapt attention: Fr von Küenburg, professor of Ethics, at Jōchi (Sophia University), then a small, all-male college with barely five hundred students, yet affectionately known to all of us. Fr von Küenburg, an Austrian aristocrat by birth, spoke quietly but with great conviction. I still remember one sentence: 'If you want to work in Japan, come with the conviction that you can learn as much from them as they from you.'

He cited an example of Japanese sensibility. Once he had

called up a student who was obviously unprepared. He, the teacher, had shown his displeasure by frowning, but had not said a thing. The following day, he found in his mail-box an apology and an answer to yesterday's question in excellent German. I was impressed, as I was every time I heard or read anything about the Japanese.

A Japanese young man would find the life of a novice even more acceptable than I did as a European. Many Japanese like living in a group or, shall we say, used to until of late when the atmosphere in the country is beginning to change in the direction of more and more individualism. I learned a lot in these years on the art of *kyōdō-seikatsu* (living together). I wish I had then known more of the unspoken rules which govern Japanese group life. The hardest thing for the average European is to subordinate the individual to the whole. Instinctively he wants his way. Religious societies are the nearest thing in the Western world to approach the Japanese mode of life. Regard for the whole is stressed far more than self-importance, and fame far less than self-effacement.

Such virtues we learned not so much from the Master's lectures as from each other. Young men of various backgrounds but animated by the same ideals, undistracted by the search for a wife or a job, full of good spirits and ready to make jokes and laugh – this compensates for other deprivations.

Still, I was glad when the two years of noviciate were over. I had occasional bouts of *ennui*. Apart from books on the spiritual life, on the history of the Church and the Jesuit Order, on medieval and modern mysticism and the like, there was nothing much to read. Nor did I feel the intellectual challenge of academic life about which my former classmates, now at the university, would growingly talk on coming for a visit. They, on the contrary, would envy me my very austerity. One of them, a brilliant Law student at Bonn University, later entered the same noviciate.

After the noviciate, we moved on to study first philosophy,

then theology, in the House of Studies of Valkenburg, situated just across the border in Holland, some ten kilometres from Aachen, one of the oldest German towns. The college's scholarly reputation was among the highest among Jesuit academic institutions, and young men from all over the world flocked together there. The most stimulating time in my mental development then began. I penetrated much more deeply into the world of my Jesuit life by studying with Jesuit comrades, but also made my first serious contact with other languages and civilizations. I spent part of the following years in France, part of them in England, and ended up, at the end of seven years, in Japan.

During the first of these eight years I met my first Japanese Jesuit, Takemiya Hayato, later for many years *Kōchō* (head) of Rokkō Kōtōgakkō (high school). By several years my senior (*sempai*), he had the qualities I respect most in the Japanese: warm-heartedness, a capacity for listening, discernment in human relations and politeness. In short, he knew when to speak and when to be silent. This statement does not contradict his habit as *kōchō* to give interminable speeches. Some of the stories about him are, no doubt, humorously exaggerated. Thus it is said that, at *chōrei* (morning assembly), he would go on talking until the first pupil fainted and fell to the ground. But when addressing a large audience, he was lengthy and eloquent because he thought he had an important message to convey. I have heard from many that, indeed, he created a lasting impression. I have never heard any criticisms about him. In those younger days he wrote a book in German: *Die Seele Japans* (The soul of Japan). I am glad that, some forty years later, I was able to incorporate feelings similar to his in a book with a similar title *Wakon Yōkon* (Japanese spirit, Western spirit) by way of *ongaeshi* (repaying a favour) as I wrote to him.

Another Japanese I became a friend of was Oizumi Takashi, later to be president of Jōchi (Sophia). We called him 'Jimmy'. We were then not aware that the *Oijime* we heard when he introduced himself was really the Tōhoku (north-east Japan) pronunciation of *Oizumi*. What impressed me then, as well as through all the many years we later worked together at Jōchi, was his real love for Germany. He always found something to praise or to excuse about the Germans. I remember seeing him once engaged in a heated argument with a young Irishman who apparently had been voicing grievances about 'the Germans'. 'No, no, no,' he kept saying, 'you don't understand them.' I am not a chauvinist, but, like many other men, I love to hear my nation thought of well by other nationals. One should voice criticism of one's own country not of others' motherland.

Of the Fathers in charge of my training as professors and advisers, some influenced me deeply, others only in a more superficial manner. At any rate, I have never known, in the nine years till I was ordained a priest, a single Father whom I could not admire. And it must be remembered that they were all living with us under the same roof, so we knew them well.

The man who made the deepest impact on me was also the first I met upon leaving the noviciate. Fr Wilhelm Klein was 'Spiritual Adviser'. A man in that position has to deliver an occasional lecture on the religious life and to be ready for personal discussion (*mi-no-ue-sōdan*). I went to his room to introduce myself and immediately felt in the presence of a truly generous priest, who also was an intellectual. He could take one seriously, and when answering he could tell a good story or even crack a good joke, but always convey a thought on which to ponder. Nobody backed me more strongly than he in my wish to go to Japan. This first talk was very different from the rather tense and solemn tone of our novice master. In fact, our first conversation was partly about the noviciate, and the unavoidable need for the novice to cut attachment to the world. 'The rest of your life, however, won't be that of a novice with blinkers, unless you make it so,' he said. With the intuitive power of a twenty-year-old, I took this sentence as a programme for my life. *Mekakushi* (blindfold) is *Scheuklappe* in

German. The slogan came to mean for me that, as a priest, I need not shut my eyes to the world. And 'Christian humanism' means just that. It was the idea the founder of the Jesuits, Ignatius of Loyola, shared with his contemporaries in Renaissance Europe such as with Erasmus and Thomas More.

Once or twice a week, in the evening, Fr Klein would give us a quiet talk of half an hour by way of help for the morning meditation. It would be around a biblical text, or a church festival, a saint's day, or a point of theology or morals. In a calm voice, as if speaking to himself, he would reflect on things of the faith, without any unctuousness or mawkishness. He had a disarming way of turning expressions around so that they acquired a new meaning. *Philosophia perennis* means 'everlasting', and was used for Scholasticism. He would say jokingly *verjährt* (superannuated) and thus encouraged us to be detached and critical.

He would say: 'Many of you may now be thinking, "What's the use of making the resolution to break a bad habit. I've tried it often, and never carried it out. I give up." Don't say that. This afternoon I went through the garden. I saw that old pear tree, you know, near the brook. For years now that tree has never brought forth fruit. But each spring it blooms rejoicing the hearts of the beholder. So your resolution may in the end not be carried out, but, like a blossom, it will still be a pleasure to God and man.'

Several years ago, invited as visiting professor to Tübingen University, Professor Eschenburg introduced me to his colleague, the famous Theology Professor Küng. Küng said to me in the course of a brief conversation: 'It was a Jesuit who changed my life. You may not even know him, Fr Wilhelm Klein. Without him I would have remained a common-or-garden-variety theologian.' Like many others, I do not agree with some of Küng's propositions, and certainly not with his manner of proposing them. But, again like many others, I am grateful to him for having re-stated basic religious questions in the way modern man would find intelligible.' I can well see Fr

Klein fostering in a budding theologian the thought that dogma must constantly be newly interpreted as the *Zeitgeist* (spirit of the times) develops. In that same way I learned from him to affirm lovingly the variety of human experience in different languages and cultures.

I was taught by men of learning and piety, respect for the freedom of their students, and usually well aware of real life outside our cloistered house. All of them had their doctorate either from German, British or French universities or from the Gregorian University in Rome. I retain vivid memories of every one of them, but shall mention here only a few. Fr Wasmann, the famous pioneer in the study of ant society, a friendly, ever courteous old man, was still alive. The similarly famous psychologist Fröbes was my teacher. And I heard two condensed lecture series on world literature by Professor Overmans, the last foreign *sennin kyōju* (senior professor) at Tokyo Imperial University. I have never listened to a man of such immense knowledge, and so generous in sharing it with his students. Nakano Shigeharu praises him for being the only one to have stood by him in the red-witch hunt of the early Shōwa period, which began in 1926.

Father du Blic was professor of ethics during my studies abroad (*ryūgaku*) in France. His thinking was permeated by gentleness, compassion and generosity, in short the qualities that distinguish the Bible from a law book. He made us see that ethics is concerned not only with abstract principles but with living and irrational reality. 'Most of our moral dilemmas are not choosing between good and evil, but between bigger and lesser good, or between bigger and lesser evil,' he would say. I also remember: 'No doubt, a man must love his mother, but must he love her at the sacrifice of his wife's happiness?' Once I submitted to him a report on colonialism, a sharply critical piece, easy to write for a German, since we had just lost our colonies. He gave me undeservedly good marks. But he added these words: 'Have a little pity on the poor French. How are they to get rid of their colonies overnight? There is more involved than your abstract idealism.' His attitude represented what I later came to know as *nasake* (compassion). The Japanese, as I have meanwhile found out, do respect ethical principles. But they equally stress an individual's concrete character and his concrete environment. This attitude is very much in the tradition of the Society of Jesus. The Jesuits are often accused of 'casuistry'. What they really mean is: ethics practised 'case by case'. It is for this highly humane ideal that they are accused of laxism by their enemies.

Theology, as then taught in Valkenburg, followed a rigorously philological and historical methodology. Such famous professors as Fr Lange or Fr Rabeneck were men of formidable knowledge and it was no easy matter to marshall the stuff of their lectures for reports and examinations. Neither at London University nor at Nancy University did I have to work as hard as in the German theologate. Still we were all dedicated students, and not to fall asleep as Rabeneck ('Raben' is the English raven) monotonously lectured could call for heroism. I still remember a comic poem composed in those days by a fellow student; the rough meaning was this:

> A murmuring brook and the nightingale
> A snoring class and the murmuring raven

Fr Prüm was, with all his unpredictable whims, a most inspiring teacher in the field of comparative religion. He began publishing his treatises on the encounter of early Christianity and Hellenism while I was his student. I understand they are still indispensable in the field. He had a disconcerting habit of beginning his lecture at the point where he had stopped thinking in his room. Often he had to be asked to specify what he was talking about. I remember him with special gratitude because of the encouragement he gave me with my dissertation on 'Resurrection' in the Isis-Osiris Myth. In those days the Jesuit colleges considered of an academic level consistent with that of the Gregorian University in Rome were entitled to bestow the doctoral degree. Valkenburg was in that category and there I obtained my doctorate. The system was abolished some time ago, as indeed much else has changed. In my time, and for a long time after, the lectures in the principal fields of philosophy and theology were conducted in Latin, and so were the main examinations. I feel no regret that this is no longer the case, although I profited much from speaking Latin fluently. A language now dead, which was at no time much extended beyond Europe and Latin America, cannot properly be a vehicle for expressing the existential problems of philosophy or a theology intelligible to modern man.

I have qualms about the abolition of Latin in Mass. There was something mystical in the old classical liturgy, and in this *yūgen*[12] (elegant simplicity) the sentiment of piety grows. Hilaire Belloc in his *Path to Rome* describes how having walked the night through the Alps, he arrives in the morning in a valley as the bells ring from the companile to indicate the hour of Mass. He goes and kneels down with the small group of villagers, and what moves him is precisely that he hears little but is enveloped in a sacred silence. The present Japanese version of the liturgy produces occasionally a vulgar effect, as when *bungotai* (written Japanese) is awkwardly and unnecessarily mixed with *kōgotai* (colloquial Japanese) or metaphors, unintelligible in Japanese, are translated when they should have been exchanged or dropped. Perhaps the Japanese language itself is changing and we have to wait for things to settle. When, some years ago, I was very despondent about these sudden changes and talked to a Buddhist monk, a friend of mine, he consoled me:

> You should not despair. At least your religionists have tried to adapt to modern times. Look at our rites. We have not changed a thing in a thousand years. And now nobody, not even an educated believer, knows any more what these recitations mean, or the incense, the candles, the bells, the drums. We have become a funeral religion.

This may all be true. Still, an element of mysticism should remain in worship. No doubt, if religion presents itself as too recondite, the ordinary believer in our hectic present will either turn to some fanatical and simplistic substitute new religion or else abandon religion altogether.

When I joined the Jesuits, I was not fully aware of the international contacts I was about to make, thanks to the Order.

Many Japanese, especially nowadays, are ostensibly worried about their supposed lack of internationality. I personally think that few other nations provide so much knowledge about foreign countries as are offered in this country through school curricula, mass media, books and – of late – even *manga* (cartoons). What the Japanese do not have is the opportunity to enter into living contact with foreigners. It was my good fortune to meet as my first Japanese two young men who were one with us in mind and heart. Takemiya spoke excellent German, Oizumi fluent if somewhat faulty German. It was not language, but the feeling for and the knowledge about their hosts that made them so attractive. They remained throughout very Japanese, decorously smiling all the time, as if they were representing their nation. But still they accepted us and we them on the same level – where common problems can be unreservedly discussed, and common jokes laughed about without commentary. Few Japanese can manage that, but for the simple reason that they lack the opportunity of intimate acquaintance with a foreigner, in other words of his value system.

Having been accepted as a volunteer for work in Japan, I asked to be sent to study for a year or so in an English S.J. House of Studies. I had discovered that most serious books about Japan, and all the valuable grammars and dictionaries, were published in English and that English was by far the most widely known foreign language in the Far East. But there were no vacancies in the English Philosophate. So my Superior suggested that I go to France, where, it turned out, he had already made inquiries. I accepted, of course, but not too gladly. I did not see the need for French in my future work in Japan and, ever since the post-war misery, I did not feel particularly attracted to France. It is true that I did cherish from the time of my youth happy memories of friendship with French boys met on hiking tours. Still, I accepted the offer. And I must now state, that the year in France was extremely rewarding and proved decisive for my later development. I discovered – as I should have foreseen – that the French people were rather different from their politicians. I also discovered – and this I could not have foreseen – that it was possible, and indeed rather easy, to master another language more or less perfectly in a comparatively short time. A final thing I discovered concerned my outlook on life. The stolid German way of looking up to authority, of conforming with those around one and of considering criticism of the authorities a fault rather than a virtue, all that was not the only way of being a Christian or a European. Not that these were entirely new insights. But what I had learned from my own family and from the persons in the Order whom I most respected until now, was confirmed by my French experience. All the same, the dangers of a pronouncedly individualistic view of life became equally apparent to me. The French are 'dry', certainly when compared with the 'wet' Germans. Germans do like a warm atmosphere and are a little bit sentimental, eager to make everybody – not only a few – happy. That is *Gemütlichkeit* (friendly informality). Here humour thrives, while the French rather cultivate *esprit* which contributes to witty conservation but not necessarily to pleasant togetherness.

In our German houses of study we found relaxation (apart from sports), – in those days without hi-fi, or electric guitars and combos – in community singing, fireside choruses, marionettes and an occasional classic orchestra or an oratorio for Christmas. The young French, on the contrary, tended invariably to be classical or else they stayed away from music completely; that was the majority. To this day the *chanson* is 'consumers' music. It is not much actively performed. I joined a singers' group. My French friends spurned the German folk songs I had proposed to teach, but preferred the contrapuntal hymns of Josquin des Près[13] or the chorals of Bach. I was glad to be admitted to their select group. But I also felt that the very selectiveness also implied divisiveness. The French do not crave, as do the Germans and Japanese, consensus and conformity.

The entertainment on major feast days in our community similarly followed exclusive patterns. After dinner there would be a well-set speech, construed according to the rules of rhetoric by Bossuet, an equally elegant piece of poetry, eliciting appreciative smiles from the professors and the leading students, and then we would lift our glass of cognac, with a bow to each other, for a final toast.

With us in Germany the plebian puppet play was the high point of the carnival season, whereas the young student priests in France produced, with almost professional precision, a classical theatre piece. I think in the year I was there it was Racine's *Bérénice.* Years later, when I conducted a seminar in the (Jōchi) *Daigakuin* (post graduate school) following Auerbach's *Mimesis,* I once looked for a copy of this drama in order to correct Auerbach's excessive criticism of Racine and the *Grand Siècle* in general. I discovered the line which brought back to me that unforgettable performance, some fifty years ago, by my young French fellow Jesuits. It is the scene where Emperor Titus declaims to the Jewess whom he has brought with him from Palestine that he cannot marry her for reasons of state. Auerbach rejects the literature of the *Grand Siècle* as sterile, because it is rhetorical and unreal. But that this condemnation is excessive, can be seen in this passage. Bérénice interrupts the grandiloquent protestations of Titus with the simple words: *Je vous croirais, Seigneur, sur un simple soupir* (I would believe you, Sire, even if you just sighed). This sentence alone makes the story truly human, totally independent from theories on rhetorical and unreal devices. Bérénice calmly accepts her fate:

her love is reciprocated but cannot lead to lasting union. To express such intense feelings in a very few words, I came to learn later, is typical rather of such Japanese writers as Natsume Sōseki[14] or Kawabata Yasunari,[15] or indeed of much Japanese literature. One is reminded also of Goethe. In *Faust*, Gretchen, at a similar desperate parting scene, has only this to say:

> *Denkt Ihr an mich ein Augenblickchen nur;*
> *Ich werde Zeit genug an Euch zu denken haben.*
>   (Think of me only for a little while;
>   I shall have time enough to think of you.)

Much of our free time we spent talking. The French are great talkers, always ready to propose a theory, or defend a cause. But in order to be accepted into their conversation, the stranger has to master their language; otherwise he is simply ignored. The Germans have far more patience with outsiders, indeed, they are flattered to be asked to help. So are the Japanese, although, even if asked, they will refrain from correcting the mistakes of others, for fear, perhaps, of being thought impolite. At any rate, within a month I knew enough to follow lectures, and after another month or two, I could listen and speak almost like a native.

What was this success due to? First of all, I followed the old-fashioned method of thoroughly studying grammar again from the beginning: I managed to read, write and translate as much as possible – much of that before arriving in France. In France, I started with conversation. But to the end of my stay I read about a book a week, and I always had good friends to correct my written pieces. I must stress, however, that I had several big assets: I was twenty, and it is a well-known fact that after this age the power of retention declines. In addition, I knew Latin, that is to say I could not only read, but even write and speak it. Lastly, I have a gift for languages, that is to say, I am fascinated by languages and I have the musical ear and the talent for mimicry essential for success in hearing and speaking. My German companion (no longer with us), a very serious and studious young man, was at home with books rather than people; he was shy and reticent, tried hard, blushed when making a mistake, and never overcame that halting hesitancy which the French so dislike. One should never underestimate the influence of personal temperament in acquiring foreign languages. That is the reason why I have certain reservations concerning excessive emphasis on drill, tapes and cassettes or the 'total immersion' method, nowadays in vogue. The Japanese take it terribly to heart that, as a whole, they do not master foreign languages. But how should it be otherwise with so homogeneous and insular a people? Electronics is some help but not the answer. Only living in a foreign milieu can make a person fluent in that language. Meanwhile, the painstaking task of analysing sentences and learning grammatical rules and plenty of words will remain the principal task in the schools. Learning a language can also provide a splendid means to form character and intelligence.

I had been warned in Germany not to speak of politics while in France. I might as well have been forbidden to speak of the weather. My generation, both French and German, was full of grievances about the post-war [World War I] settlement, blaming each other for the impasse. The French point of view was that German nationalism was still rampant, thirsting for revenge and as a proof they might well point to the 113 seats which Hitler's followers had won in the election of the summer of 1930. It was the very summer I arrived and I remember my embarassment when, during my first days in France one of the editors of the Paris S.J. monthly gave to us students an analysis of Hitler's first crushing victory in an election. He was well informed. He predicted that the Nazis might come to power – which I would not have considered possible. He also failed to connect Nazi success with the economic depression. The bleak economic climate was much worse in Germany than elsewhere, and we Germans thought it had become aggravated by French intransigence.

The German point of view was that the unfair Treaty of Versailles would make possible the rise of resentment and thus of Hitler. The Japanese reaction would have been to let these two 'standpoints' stand side by side, not take sides and proceed to other matters. Not so French and Germans. They must argue and argue, not for argument's sake nor for self-righteousness, but because of the assumption that of two opposing views only *one* can be right. Fortunately, none of us ever lost his temper; furthermore, each one of us learned some fact or circumstance he had not known before and finally we got tired of the subject. I drew the important moral that, despite my endeavour to adapt to another culture, I was still full of prejudices which I mistakenly considered objective truths. I know that my friend de Roton – later to be an influential teacher and writer in South India – came to think similarly about himself. A common world view, the common pursuit of learning, and our day-long hikes into the Cevennes Mountains made us a happy community. I left it with sadness. I spent that whole summer at the University of Nancy where I obtained a diploma for '*enseignement de langue et littérature françaises a l'étranger*' (teaching French language and literature to foreigners) with the mark '*Très bien, avec mention spéciale de phonétique*'. (Very good, with special commendation for the understanding of phonetics.)

I returned to our German house of Studies to finish my theology. My French experience had been brief but intense. It was to last, not only for the remaining period of studies. The encounter had made me aware of the moral element in cultural interaction. An element of self-abnegation is needed. Germans in France are likely to complain of lack of warm feeling. They should, instead, reflect on their own sentimentalism. Thus, there are many foreign residents in Tokyo who complain about Japanese secretiveness which they describe as dishonest or arrogant. They should rather learn from the Japanese regard for other people's feelings. Again Japanese abroad, if too naïvely attached to the niceties of life at home, will never come to appreciate another civilization, be it its bread and wine or its religion, philosophy and literature.

Still, a man has only one fatherland. I myself, cosmopolitan as I have become in half a century abroad, still consider myself a German first, although by now I prefer occasional visits home to living there permanently. Ever since my year with the French, my love of Germany has acquired the characteristics of what, in Japanese, is called *yūkoku*: grief for German shortcomings, for dangers besetting her. It was then that I came to think in European rather than nationalist terms. My father's musings from the time of my childhood were maturing in me: 'We must enlarge our horizon.'

The final years of studying theology were strenuous, but I kept up the custom acquired in France of reading one book in one or two weeks outside the field of theology proper. I managed to re-read much German verse and prose, besides keeping up with French. I was playing with the idea of taking up Russian. But our Russian expert among the theology students advised me against. I would not have the time, he said, and instead he urged me to read all the great Russians available in translation. I did this under his guidance and am eternally grateful to him for opening a new world. Fr Roos, who was a few years older than I, later went to Copenhagen, where he had the chair at the National University for medieval mysticism. I met him for the last time in Paris in 1956 at an international meeting of Jesuit editors. Like the publication *Sophia*, which I had founded in Tokyo, so the magazine he was editing in Copenhagen was mainly concerned with problems of comparative culture. Fr Roos – as full of pep and vitality as he had been twenty years before – told me in Paris of his adventure which had made him famous in Europe. A year or so before, he had been invited as a visiting professor to the University of Upsala. He submitted his curriculum vitae, and thus the Ministry of Education at Stockholm discovered that he was a Jesuit. He received notice that according to the Swedish Constitution, no Jesuit was admitted to the country, but that, of course, in his case an exception would be made. He was welcome, but he must observe one condition: see the police every day (or was it every week?) while in the country. Roos replied that, sorry, under these conditions he would not come at all. This was reported in the Swedish press and then in all European mass media – few people had been aware that so narrow-minded a prejudice from the time of Gustavus Adolphus[16] and the religious wars was still enacted as law. Parliament quickly voted to do away with the shameful paragraph. The shock became one of the reasons why Switzerland also, the last European country with such bigotted legislation, later officially admitted Jesuits as citizens.

At the end of my theology studies, I had my long-awaited first chance to go to England. From the time of my childhood, when friendly officers of the occupation army had talked to me, I had felt familiar with English and, later, although little English was taught at Gymnasium, I had learned to read it with ease. There were also several Americans among my fellow students in Valkenburg with whom I had started to practise conversation. One of them, a veritable humorist, Maderras, later to go to a Baghdad university run by the American Jesuits, volunteered to practise spoken English with a group of us on Saturday afternoons. It was his first experience in teaching English. He became so impatient at the unsuspected inconsistencies in English pronunciation that he began to mimeograph a text for us, entitled 'Rules on Pronouncing English'. But, as he told us in his incomparable *rakugo* (Japanese story-teller) manner, he had to abandon the project. 'English has no rules. English is silly. I pity you,' he said, wiping away feigned tears, and we laughed. Of course, no language is silly. Still, as I now began to delve single-mindedly into the English language while living with English people, I discovered that English is easy only at first sight. It is a simple thing to pick up the first few expressions and talk of the weather or go out shopping. But as you proceed, it gets harder and harder. There are few rules for grammar and pronunciation and the vocabulary is double that of any other European language. The result is that few non-native speakers succeed in writing a faultless letter, let alone essay, or delivering an impeccable after-dinner speech. Yet in German, French and most other European languages that can be done. In contrast to English, the beginning is hard, but as you advance it gets easier.

I passed my *dai-san-shūren* (third year of religious training) in St Bruno's, Wales – a massive medieval monastery situated among beautiful, woody hills. This last period in the formation of a Jesuit is placed at the end of his studies before he plunges into action. It is one year added to the two years of noviciate with which he began. The idea is to renew the spirit of devotion in an atmosphere of silence and community warmth. By and large, these aims were achieved. Yet, as in my first two years of noviciate so now I often felt a little bored. As I understand, *dai-san-Shūren* has, in the course of the many Church reforms during the last two decades, come to change. The exercises of piety are blended with a few weeks of work in parishes or field study (*kengaku*), and perhaps that is a good thing.

We were a group of about forty; besides the majority of English, a large contingent of Irish and a few men from other countries. The English are, by and large, a phlegmatic race. Their interests are few, and foreigners or foreign things are certainly not among them. I had not expected that the English Jesuits were so very 'English' in much of their behaviour. Our Father Instructor spoke to us almost daily on our life as priests, pastors or teachers and he often remarked: 'Gentlemen, don't dig yourselves in for a comfortable life.' It is definitely not the kind of advice to give to French or German young men preparing to be priests. On the contrary, they will have to be warned against working too hard in order to avoid stomach ulcers.

The Instructor was Fr Geddes, a Scotsman, friendlily

disposed to all of us, a model priest and Jesuit, but neither eager nor able to convey to us his inner convictions. One felt he would have been happiest on the golf course with a couple of equally taciturn Scotsmen.

Once during my stay, Fr Lassalle – who later became naturalized in Japan and adopted the name Enomiya Makibi – came to pay me a visit. He was Superior of the Jesuits in Japan. He also went to see Fr Geddes, the Instructor, who warmly welcomed him and said, 'Sit down and tell me all about Japan'. Fr Enomiya proceeded to tell, circumstantially and in detail, 'all' about Japan, and after a while, Fr Geddes was fast asleep, and stayed so until the gong for dinner sounded.

My year in England had little in common with the year in France. No hectic discussions, no conversations on art, literature or music, no talk about politics – never mind the fact that Hitler was a dark cloud on the horizon. Indeed, when after each meal, we dispersed into the vast garden for a walk and for talks, the English would wherever possible avoid going with foreigners. Not from motives of haughtiness but from a mixture of phlegm and laziness, but also shyness: they instinctively avoid meeting others, especially strangers. There were exceptions; one of them, Fr Corbishley, was a fast friend and great helper to me years later when I returned to England from Japan for studies at London University. Without his help I would have been unable to translate Ariwara no Narihira's *tanka* (Japanese short poem) into 5–7 English trochaic rhythms.

My partners in conversation were mostly the Irish Fathers. There must have been seven or eight of them and they were all equally affable, thoughtful and interested in a foreigner's views. I was so often in their company that I must have picked up part of their accent without being aware of it. English as spoken by educated Irishmen is beautiful, clearer and more melodious than the slurring South-English variety or the harsh Midlands' voice. Thanks to the Irish influence I never acquired the excessive dipthong pronunciation of the so-called Oxbridge dialect.

Irish-English is the best middleway between British-English and American-English. To keep from both extremes is quite a plus in the atmosphere of Japan. In fact, on some of this middle ground many foreign instructors teach English in Japan, whether by design or from necessity.

By the autumn of 1935, I was set for the ultimate step in my inter-cultural adventure story – the trip to Japan. The image of Japan had been looming in my motives to join the Jesuit Order. During my years of education in the Order, and in the midst of my intimate contacts with various cultures, that image had grown. The year, in which my desire to go to Japan was finally to be fulfilled, was overshadowed by stirrings of totalitarianism in both Germany and Japan. Hitler had taken over in Germany, and Japan was in the midst of the Manchurian (*Manshū*) Incident. It was with a certain trepidation that I travelled to Berlin in September to board the Trans-Siberian Express.

I had come to know a number of European capitals but this was my first visit to the capital city of my own country. I found it built with wide and open avenues and with practical precision, but somewhat cold and aggressive. My father's prejudices against *nouveau-riche* Berlin, no doubt, played their part. In addition the city had, in two years, become the chief citadel of Hitlerism. Arrogantly marching storm-troopers, swastika (*Hakenkreuz*) flags all over, martial music over the loudspeakers – having mostly been abroad, or among the gentle Rhinelanders, the horror of what had befallen my beloved country came down on me with a bang, in the very last days before leaving the country.

I remember one shock. I had always succeeded in avoiding having to make the Hitler salute. But one day as I left the Ministry of Foreign Affairs where I had my passport endorsed, all of a sudden, as I turned a corner in the cavernous building, a tall man in brown uniform raised his hand and shouted in a stentor voice, 'Heil Hitler!'. Quite instinctively I did the same, motivated, no doubt, by a mixture of panic and automatism. I was ashamed of myself. This was the only time I ever did it. Still it would be unfair to boast. True, I had not bowed to the *fuwa raidō* (blindly following) spirit then already prevailing. But I did not have to live on under Nazi pressure. I was soon to be outside.

We travelled via Warsaw, Moscow, Tomsk etc. and along the Baikal Lake, to Japanese-occupied Manchuria, then through Korea to take a ferry-boat which brought us early in the morning to Shimonoseki. I shall never forget the azure sky of a veritable *Nihonbare* (clear autumn) October day, the white sailing boats in the blue sea, and the busy, smiling, neat-looking people in the narrow streets. The two weeks of travel through Asia had been depressing in their monotony, sad and undernourished people standing at every station, the symbol of the 'workers paradise' being the omnipresent armed militia men. All that was forgotten the moment I trod on Japanese soil. I felt, having left Europe two weeks ago, I was now back in Europe, or something similarly alive, eager, energetic.

From the first day I trod the soil of the country I felt welcomed, and have felt so ever since. For my part, I have felt real affection for this people and it increased, the longer I stayed. Much as I have never lost my affection for Germany, I say this here on purpose. My attachment to both my home country and my host country were soon to be tested. Totalitarianism was to establish itself in both Germany and Japan, and I was to witness the sorry spectacle in both countries as well as in England, the last bastion of democracy, as she looked at the time. But this is another chapter in my life between cultures: after two years' language study in Japan, I returned to England for academic work. There I watched the outbreak of the Hitler war in Europe, and, on my return to Japan, I watched Pearl Harbor and its consequences.

CHAPTER THREE

Tokyo – London. Slithering into the War

— oOo —

H aving read all available books about Japan, not much was to surprise me as I arrived at last in October 1935. But I had not expected the almost poetical quality of life I encountered. Through the train windows on the Sanyō and Tōkaidō lines I saw the coves and paddies of the Japan of Hiroshige; and the people in the train were as gentle and friendly as on the prints. One peculiar phenomenon that has survived both the war and the present lengthy material prosperity are the clusters of teenage girls, always giggling and nodding at each other as they recount their interminable stories.

I knew from the newspapers of the Manchurian Crisis. But I felt no electric tension in the air. That was the big difference to Germany. In fact, the way democracy crumbled differently in different countries was a decisive experience in those years.

Meanwhile, my entire energy was consumed by learning the language. I stayed in the religious house, down the slope from

Kōjimachi to Akasaka. It was quiet yet near the city centre. I did not attend a language school. I followed my own pace with a tutor. I was convinced from my experience with language learning that you either learn it with great intensity or you do not learn it at all. One must aim at reaching as quickly as possible, the point of enjoying the 'feel' and the aroma of the new language. Fortunately, I had become fond of the soft accent and intonation of Japanese in a relatively short time. I found that the language is accommodating and tolerant. No language is spoken with quite the precision of its grammar, and Japanese even less. No doubt, that leads to ambiguity, but that is the very charm. I was to find out much later that the Japanese aversion to bluntness and insistence makes life in Japan so pleasant. As I was learning by heart daily conversational texts from the grammar by Rose-Innes and had my intonation corrected in the gentle inflections of my tutor Watanabe, soon to die in the war, I felt my life entering into a new *fluidum*. Japanese is a civilized language, hence it is reticent, understated and reserved.

One way of relaxing then, as still today, was strolling through the streets of Tokyo. In Kanda I soon discovered Tokyo's *Rive Gauche*, although there was little I could as yet read. But one momentous discovery I was able to make in those days, a small book by Arthur Waley[17] called *Uta*, offering a number of *Tanka*[18] (short poem) from the *Manyōshū*[19] and the *Kokinshū*[20] in both word-for-word translation and an English poetical reconstruction. This Japanese I could recognize with the help of my very modest vocabulary of those days. It confirmed my theory about the quiet elegance of the language.

The *kanji* (Chinese characters), I thought, were rather easy to learn. The only thing I had done in Europe by way of preparation had been an intensive study of the way they are structured, *hen* (radical) and *tsukuri* (additional part), and I had learned by heart the 214 'radicals', from *ichi* (one) to *kame* (tortoise). When travelling from Shimonoseki by train, this knowledge had helped me little when looking up in the *Kan'ei-Jiten* (dictionary of Chinese characters with English translations) place names especially advertising, like the ubiquitous *Jintan* (a lozenge) or *Daigaku Megusuri* (literally university medicine for eyes). Now I was able to proceed with a certain speed. I soon forced myself to read the newspaper in Japanese, I also began to dip into the monthly reviews.

I did a lot of forcing myself. I would walk on the roof in the sun without sitting down, until I had learned 12 characters: reading, writing, pronouncing *on* (Chinese reading of a character) and *kun* (Japanese reading of a Chinese character) and translating. Or again, I would walk a street until I could read every single public notice. One main subject of the final examination was to know the *tōyō kanji* (Chinese characters prescribed for daily use). Another point was the ability to improvise a conversation, based on two texts to be read aloud: a news item from a newspaper or a current monthly and from some modern book. This examination was to be taken after two years. I summoned the courage to try after one year; I am sure I made a lot of mistakes. I distinctly remember having forgotten both reading and meaning of *zei* (taxation). But I passed.

My idea of trying the examination earlier than usual had been to escape from Tokyo with its too numerous foreign contacts and go to Japanese surroundings. The Fathers had several parishes in the Sanyō District. There I would have more opportunity to practise the spoken language. It turned out as I had hoped, or rather, better than I had hoped. For I had barely arrived in Hiroshima, when I was requested to help teaching at Hiro-Kō (school), until the arrival of the newly contracted German *kyōshi* (teacher). There could not have been a more felicitous event than these few months of proximity with academic Japanese youth at that juncture of my life.

My Japanese began to prosper. Everybody was eager to correct my Japanese essays, and especially talk to me. In class. I stuck strictly to German, also in conversation classes when requested. I learned much of the lore and language of the old style high schools (*kyūsei kōkō*). We sat around talking deep into the night – an age difference of some eight years between us. Conversation, in those blissful days, took the place now reserved to television, pachinko and motoring. Reading matter was of the Iwanami Bunko type (small paperbacks). I soon discovered that the better students had read as many European classics as European boys would have, or shall we say German boys. The French and English are not particularly interested in translated literature, then as now.

And then my students had their own classics. *Tsurezure-gusa*[21] (a famous collection of essays written in the fourteenth century by Yoshida Kenkō 1283–1330) and *Hakkenden* (a famous novel). The story of the hundred dogs by Takizawa Bakin (1767–1848) were apparently read in *kokubun* (Japanese literature) classes that year. One of my new friends told me that it took him a good hour to prepare the short passage of *Hakkenden* for the day. I was not surprised. The depressing thought overcame me: if a book contemporary to the period of Goethe could no longer be read with ease and pleasure by educated young Japanese, how could a non-Japanese fare? And what was happening to the Japanese language in general? The thought has haunted me ever since. On the one hand I passionately wish that the language will continue in that mixture of firmness and looseness which gives it its charm. On the other hand I am worried by a steady and uninterrupted erosion. From year to year the vocabulary understood by the young goes on shrinking, grammar is forgotten or ignored, the glamour of feminine speech disappears, proverbs and idioms are no longer understood. Do we have here a peculiar Japanese phenomenon? Or are we face to face with the distinctive influence on the continuity of any language by the impact of the second industrial revolution?

I still enjoy reading notices on my walks through Tokyo. Occasionally, I also stop at Yasukuni shrine; there, entering the inner shrine, every week or so, is placed the letter by some young officer to his parents or *kyōdai* (fellow students) the day before his death in the field. I admire the terseness of the *sōrōbun* (classical style), *Chichiue yo!* (honourable father) ... How garrulous can modern Japanese be in contrast! It is turning into a jargon for the telephone, I often feel.

I read these letters as an admirer of the Japanese language, not for ethical reasons, since I cannot always share their self-righteous chauvinism. I admit, I also admire the obvious genuineness of the content. It reminds me of the old Hiroshima. About half of my students in *Bun-Otsu* (second class in literature studies) and *Ri-Otsu* (second class in scientific studies) died in the war, and of these, quite a few – but probably less than half – died with simple and austere sentiments of patriotism, a kind of filial patriotism, deep attachment to the household of Japan, and its father the Emperor. I say this not because of what people then told me, but of what, by and by, I found out. Politics is not as passionately debated by the Japanese as it is by Europeans. The Japanese face politics with the attitude of facing a natural disaster, an earthquake or a typhoon. There is not much one can do about it. Certainly, the atmosphere in the Germany which I had just left was different.

Politics is the very stuff of conversation in Western Europe. Even today I find it disagreeable to be around in Germany when an election comes up, because the air is so tense. In the days when Hitler came to power the debate was shrill, incessant and, indeed, ruthless. Armed bands of terrorists of extreme left and right fought on the streets and in factories and lecture halls until, finally, an election was held. The issue was, by 1933, clear: Hitler, yes or no. Now he was already in a coalition cabinet. He had enough power to harass opposition politicians. Yet with all the odds in his favour, Hitler did not obtain an absolute majority. The seats won by a conservative party helped him to the necessary 51 per cent. His party alone had not made it. Still within a year or two he could count on the support of the masses. By way of terror he silenced any opposition, and by shrewd but unsound economic policy he stopped unemployment. When I said goodbye to my parents on leaving for Japan, my family was no longer, as it had been until 1933, typical of public opinion in our town. Neighbours and even relatives were beginning to believe in, what my father called sarcastically, 'the new saviours'.

In Japan, the growth of totalitarianism followed different rules. There was little terrorism; there were elections, but they did not determine events. The year after I first came, in January 1936, moderate political parties had won a surprising majority against the militarists, four months after I arrived. But the horrible event one month later, the [*ni-ni-roku jiken*] (the 26 February Incident), nullified the election in a way nobody could explain to me at the time. I found out long after the war. The rebelling young officers did not, of course, succeed. They belonged to the *kōdō-ha* (imperial-way faction), and were crushed by the Generals of the *tōsei-ha* (control faction). The more cunning elements in the armed forces could consolidate their power. These momentous things occurred away from the public. The Japanese, in contrast to the German people, who could have read *Mein kampf,* were never asked to vote for or against further expansion in Asia, more money for the army, the transformation of *kokutai* [24] (national polity).

The final formation of a war cabinet under General Tōjō is not comparable with the advent of Hitler. Hitler's rise to power was made possible because of the acute misery of the German people caused to a considerable extent by the victors in World War I. Once he was in power, he could not be unseated. The more highly industrialized a modern nation is, the easier it is for a handful of experts to take over all posts of command. This securely installed handful of conspirers can, then, proceed and carry through the criminal plans of exterminating the Jews and preparing a major war. All this was enough justification for a War Crimes Tribunal in Nuremberg. On the other hand, none of this applied to Japan. Therefore, to put on trial Japanese leaders for a planned war and wilful atrocities was folly. The Allies had become victims of their own propaganda.

But I am anticipating. During those happy two years of studying Japanese, these islands did not look as if they were about to fall victim to a totalitarian regime as Germany was doing.

It had been decided that I should return to Europe in order to study at London University for teaching in the just-established English Literature Department of Sophia University. I bad farewell to Japan – aware that I was now inextricably 'in love' both with the country and its people – and in June 1937 sailed on a German ship out of Yokohama. Two momentous things happened on the voyage. We stayed for a day in Singapore, then a loud, untidy colonial city, full of importuning beggars and bearded Sikh policemen. Incredible contrast to the orderly, gleaming contemporary Singapore. As I strolled around, I noticed a Japanese-run coffee shop called 'Alaska'. I entered and surprised the proprietor by greeting him in Japanese. He called his wife and we chatted together, and it was they who told me that the war against China had seriously begun that day. It was 25 July 1937. None of us anticipated that the island of Singapore would soon be occupied by the Japanese and re-named Shōnantō and that its conqueror, Yamashita the Tiger, would at war's end be condemned to death by the American army, a veritable judicial murder.

The other momentous event occurred when we were sailing through the Indian Ocean. One day, I was called to the captain, and informed that the crew had lodged with him a report by eye-witnesses to the effect that I was an enemy of the State. I can only guess at what may have happened. I had become friendly with an elderly German Jew on his way back to Germany, after having sold his business in China, upon the death of his wife. He had heard of Nazi anti-Semitism, but he could not really believe it, he told me.

I told the old man with great insistence that the persecution of the Jews was certainly a central point of their programme and that it was dangerous for him to return. These repeated remarks of mine must have been overheard by informers among the crew. The captain told me he had been officially asked to submit their testimony to the Gestapo. The captain had been obliged to comply unless he was to be denounced himself, but he informed me that he would wait until the ship arrived in Bremenhaven, so that I could leave the ship in Genoa, proceeding by train to visit at least my parents in Germany on my way to England. In those days the persecution of Christian clergy was already under way. Charges were fabricated so as to discredit them with the faithful, e.g., having transported money abroad, having molested minors, having betrayed state secrets. Anyone accused was hardly able to defend himself and I was grateful to the friendly captain for having told me in time. When the police began to inquire about me, I had already left for England.

Nothing could have brought home to me with greater clarity the difference between rising totalitarianism in Germany and Japan. Compared with the devilish efficiency with which the Nazis proceeded to tackle their critics one by one, the people around Tōjō and the like were clumsy and naïve. They were not out to destroy but to convert dissidents. The Nazis had no word for *tenkō* (conversion). They had in mind *zenmetsu* (elimination). If I had been caught, I would probably have ended like many priests among my friends. When the Dachau concentration camp was liberated at war's end, Catholic priests were the largest group of inmates after the Jews.

During the few days home with my parents I had a glimpse of a Germany totally changed during an absence of two years. Only a few years ago, whenever I crossed the frontier from Valkenburg into Germany, the contrast was conspicuous between the well-nourished, nicely clad Dutch on one side, and the shabbily dressed, gaunt-looking Germans on the other: mostly unem-

ployed, standing at street corners, when not occupied with political street fights. But now people looked contented, if not exactly
happy. The 'German look' as it was ironically called, was universal: people looking first left then right before speaking to each
other. Secrecy was needed. They were being watched. I did not
tell my family, since they were facing enough hardship. My
father was already being harassed for not becoming a party member and my mother was suspected of Jewish sympathies; indeed,
a year later she was briefly arrested for having sheltered Jews during the 'cristaltnight' (*kristallnacht*) of November 1938. I left
Germany after this sad visit and for many years thereafter I felt
like Heine[25] in his French exile:

> *Denk ich an Deutschland in der Nacht,*
> *So bin ich um den Schlaf gebracht.*
> (At night I think of Germany,
> And then there is no sleep for me.)

The England I encountered in 1937 had changed little, as I
thought upon sighting gentlemen in bowler-hats and rolled-up
umbrellas, or well-dressed ladies window-shopping. But as I
enrolled at London University, I came to discover that the mental climate was highly politicized. Intellectuals and students had
come to define 'fascism' as the infamous enemy of freedom and
progress. 'Fascism' included the regimes of Hitler, Mussolini,
militaristic Japan and the Army in Spain's Civil War. Franco
especially was discussed with violence, since it looked as if his
victory in the civil war might still be prevented. In short 'fascism'
was the enemy, while it would have been more appropriate to
speak of 'totalitarianism'. But that word would have had to
include communism. This, no intellectual was inclined to do.
Many English writers (*bunkajin*, literally men of culture) were
joining the Stalinist and Trotzkiist foreign brigades fighting for
the allegedly democratic loyalist regime in Spain. To me, it had
long become clear that the two vicious totalitarian regimes to be
dreaded and resisted were those of Hitler and Stalin. I could not

bring myself to place Japan, Italy and, least of all, Spain into that category. But such things I could not discuss with my fellow students. It took some time until disillusioned poets like Auden or Spender openly spoke of the sordid treachery in the communist camp, and it took longer until they were believed. I remember the cold winter-day when, at Charing Cross, I got hold of a copy of George Orwell's[26] *Homage to Catalonia*. I began reading it in the subway and finished the book that night. I found my views vindicated, that only Stalin and Hitler represented the evil forces of the time. But some of my left-wing friends refused even to read 'that renegade', Orwell. It is hard to imagine a more sober and plainer account of the cruelty of left-wing totalitarianism than Orwell's book. But an intellectual 'fanatic's' prejudices are not easily shaken. They look for a blue-print Utopia and prefer to falsify reality rather than adapting ideals to facts. That attitude is true not only of the England or France of the time, but it became fashionable for a time in Japan as well as in Germany after World War II. Distortion of facts is always harmful; it paralyses a nation's capacity for fair judgement.

The harm done by the anti-Franco hysteria of the time turned out to be twofold. Because, as it gradually became apparent, Franco turned out far less dangerous than certain intellectuals and politicians had painted him, the man in the street came to assume that Hitler, too, was not as bad as he was made out to be. If you cry 'wolf' too often, you will not be believed when the real wolf comes. The other consequence was the portrayal of Russian Communism under Stalin as a harmless and legitimate regime. The first illusion broke down as the Hitler war began in 1939. The second one survived the war. Because at Yalta Stalin was trusted by Roosevelt as 'good old uncle Joe', the injustice was perpetuated and we still live with a divided Germany and a betrayed Eastern Europe, a divided Korea, a Japan deprived of its northern territories, and the other numerous concessions to the Soviet Empire made to 'good old uncle Joe' in Yalta.

I stayed away from political conversation in England as far as I could, not only because I was soon getting altogether too busy at the university, but especially because, too frequently, I ran into stubborn opinions which I was powerless to influence and from which I could learn little. In Japan, nobody would even try to drag me into a political discussion; in England nobody would leave me alone. At the height of the Spanish Civil War, the student climate was such that some of the most brilliant were easily recruited as spies for the USSR. Such highly placed civil servants as Philby and McLean worked against their country and fled shortly before being demasked and arrested. They were warned by the Queen's Art Consultant, Sir Anthony Blunt. Blunt, tutor at Oxford, had recruited them; the queen's adviser had himself been a spy.

I enrolled in University College, the oldest and most venerable of the constituent colleges of London University. But I was not very happy at the prospect of years of studying English language and literature together with classmates all much younger than I and all native English speakers. One day, as I was standing in the hall waiting for my turn at some *madoguchi* (window), I was spotted by the Dean of Literature with whom I had once briefly chatted, Dr Salomon, who appears in Chesterton's[27] autobiography as his best friend when both were pupils of St Paul's High School in London. He said: 'I am not happy, Father, seeing you here on the level of the undergraduates. Come into my office for a minute.' He then went with me through my academic credentials from Germany and France. When he discovered that I had studied Japanese, he exclaimed: 'Inquire at the School of Oriental and African Studies and see whether you could do your main work there, while continuing to read English here.' I did as I was told and received permission to enter the Graduate School without first acquiring a London B.A.

The Japanese department of the School turned out to have a graduate school only on paper. I was the first ever to enrol. But my two professors were just the ideal combination: one was Mr

Yoshitake, a quiet almost shy Japanese who had lived in London since World War I, and was a specialist in Japanese grammar and syntax. The other was Prof. Simon, a German Jew who had recently escaped from Berlin University. Originally his field was Sinology, but he had a wide knowledge of Japanese *kanbun* (Chinese classical style) and learned Japanese with the amazing facility so many Jews have. It was several years later after I had left, after Pearl Harbor, in fact, that the staff and library were enlarged – Arthur Waley was among those then enlisted – and the Department became the brilliant institution it now is. Still, I am grateful for having been allowed in while it was in a state of growth.

Mr Yoshitake was the most conscientious of teachers I ever had. His pedagogical skill, on the other hand, was not exactly outstanding. He had discovered that the one field where I needed to make more progress was writing. I was myself aware of this deficiency, and so I undertook with vigour the weekly Japanese essay, or translation from English into Japanese, which he stipulated. This became, however, such a burden that I ended up asking my Japanese friends, especially at the Embassy, for help. When, in due course, with outside help, I submitted a specifically demanded *sōrōbun*[28] (classical style) essay, and was highly praised, I finally broke down and confessed to my delinquency. I humbly suggested that we give up writing Japanese. I think he yielded, because he understood my reasons. Even a native Japanese, unless frequently engaged in writing, finds it difficult to write *kanji* (Chinese characters) without consulting the dictionary. For foreigners to master writing, in addition to reading, hearing and speaking, is nearly impossible.

I have known a few foreigners who can write Japanese with such a natural flow and idiomatic ease that they could pass for natives. Thus, the late Mr Hawley,[29] who came to Japan as a teacher and ended up as a special correspondent for *The Times* of London, would write letters to his Japanese wife when he was imprisoned during the early part of the Pacific War. He had no dictionary, no notes, no one to talk to, but was able to write to his Japanese wife in perfect *gyōshō* detailed orders of what he wanted done with his books and manuscripts. Still, I maintain that to correspond, take memos, write articles and books, all unaided, in Japanese, is justifiable only, if a person wants to be a Japanologist; in other words, if he concentrates on Japanese language and culture and foregoes other fields of learning. I admit that one has to be able to write, otherwise one cannot learn to read, and in that sense I did learn to write and still can write. At any rate, I personally never intended to narrow down my field of vision to Japan only. I wanted to keep abreast of philosophy, theology and world literature, hence I read much in other languages. To this day, I write Japanese only when I must. Mostly I either dictate, write in *rōmaji* or write in German or English, checking the translation meticulously.

Much of my time at the School of Oriental and African Studies went into compiling my graduation thesis. I had chosen the *Ise Monogatari* partly because I had translated sections of it with an introduction for a prize essay at the University on an 'Eastern theme', financed by some Hong Kong businessman. Prof. Ikeda Kikan of Tokyo University had just issued a variorum edition which I obtained. And my favourite Professor of English Literature at University College provided me, unwittingly, with a theme. I had heard a fascinating series of lectures by Professor R. C. Chambers, later published under the title *The Continuity of English Prose*. Chambers, a renowned authority on Sir Thomas More, the English statesman and humanist executed by King Henry VIII for opposing his divorce, convincingly shows that the English language was not disrupted by the inflow of Norman French, but kept its structure, principally because of the vigorous prose of English fifteenth-century Renaissance writers such as Thomas More. My idea was to show a similar phenomenon in Japan where the influence of the official *kambun*[30] was offset by the poets of early Heian. In the tenth century Ki no Tsurayuki[31] or Ariwara no Narihira[32]

represented a pure Yamato language still widely intact. What I
then wrote may have been correct, and to a point, perhaps even
original, but I neither had the bibliography nor the background
knowledge to write anything of lasting value. I have re-read the
paper recently and what still impresses me are the translated
poems which my old friend Corbishley, at the time editor of
the Jesuit review *The Month*, had helped me to convert into
English trochees.

As for my other principal professor, Dr Simon, I represented
to him the God-sent chance to help learn yet another language.
The *kanbun* which I then learned from him, I have all forgotten. But he was so eager to pick up Japanese and so exhilarated
by the vagaries and inconsistencies of the language as seen by a
Sinologist that, as I was told this summer, he still reads it,
although now in his eighties.

Mr Yoshitake is no longer alive, alas. I heard the story of his
sorry end when the War was over. Having lived in England for
many years, he applied for British citizenship after Pearl
Harbor, but did not find enough British friends to endorse his
petition. He deeply resented this lack of trust and soon took to
bed, as if he had decided to die. Indeed, he did soon die. But
before he did, he ordered his English wife to burn the huge
manuscript on which he had been working for so many years.
His wife sobbed while the pages went up in flames. It was an
entirely new approach to the Japanese language, but England
was not to have it. It was a great loss to learning, but I cannot
blame my teacher. It is sad to be distrusted by those one trusts.
The common friend who told me the sorry story said, at the
time: 'The British can be ruthless when they are up with their
backs against the wall.'

It is true, that England was in a desperate position being the
only power to fight Hitler in Europe. The French were
defeated. America did not intend to get involved in a European
war. Nobody continued opposing Hitler's victorious progress.
It is frightful to think of what might have happened, if Hitler

had not been prevented from having his will. And it is not to be wondered at that the British left alone could cease to be gentlemen. I personally have only grateful memories of England at her darkest hour. After having passed my final written and oral examinations at the University and, with great trouble, obtained my exit visa, I left England on 21 June 1940, a few days after the Dunkirk disaster. The British Expeditionary Force had been routed. Yet, at that very time of national humiliation, they treated me, an enemy alien, with the utmost urbanity. I had been told when granted my visa that I could not take more than a dozen books on my sea voyage to Japan, and that such books as I chose I must submit for censorship. When I showed my twelve volumes to the officials in the emigration office, they were surprised at the small quantity of reading for the long trip around the Cape of Good Hope. They offered to have my whole collection brought to the ship. In fact, they began to telephone to places in London for transport. It turned out, of course, that there was nothing available since all transport firms were busy evacuating troops from Dunkirk. Everybody apologised for being unable to help a German – in time of war!

The censor, consular and customs officers in their kindness made my farewell to Great Britain a truly sentimental affair. In general, I had made many friends during these years in England, filled with hard study and hectic politics. I had tried to keep out of politics, but I had been unable to; politics had kept up with me, in the shape of a war between my host country and me as a German guest. These precious few years would have been paradise without Hitler's war threat overshadowing them. The mood of England changed overnight on 15 March 1939, when Hitler marched into Prague and conquered Czechoslovakia in defiance of the clear promises given to Chamberlain at Munich. I myself felt as indignant at this betrayal as did the English.

One incident remains clear in my memory. In the early sum-

mer of 1939, a classmate from my days studying theology came
to London to look for assistance for German Jews whose persecution was getting increasingly systematic. He was, as a priest,
out of sympathy with the Nazi regime; furthermore as a Dutch
citizen he had a Dutch passport and so he could be expected to
be better informed about Germany than people without foreign sources of information. Yet, when I mentioned that, on 15
March public opinion had suddenly hardened in England, he
exclaimed: 'You can blame Hitler for many things, but not for
overpowering the Czechs. Why, the country was armed to the
teeth, ready to pounce upon Germany!' I was speechless. So
rapidly had the manipulation of the media by a totalitarian
propaganda machine brain-washed my old friend Fr K., a man
of my own upbringing and background, with whom I shared
the same value system.

As I said farewell to my English friends I felt I was leaving an
England, which would never be the same again. Still, I did not
foresee the depth of misery to which she would fall after a pro-
tracted war and the loss of an empire. The weakest point in the
British social structure was, I felt, the dissonance if not enmity,
between the small highly-educated sector and the big less-
educated sector, a kind of class-war based on snobbishness.
When I was in England for the first time, I was really shocked
by class-war features of the language. 'Unless you pronounce
your aitch more emphatically you will sound working class.'
'The upper-class word is not "serviette" but "napkin".' This is
how I was corrected. 'U' and 'non-U' have become accepted
terms for 'upper' and 'non-upper' (class). One would have
expected the antagonism to soften during the war for survival
and during the impoverishment of the country in post-war
years. But, while with new Comprehensive Schools and Red
Brick Universities much has improved, the basic opposition has
remained. It is an interesting subject of Comparative Culture to
contrast this University vs. non-University opposition in
England with the Paris vs. the provinces opposition in France,

and the regional vs. central oppositions in Germany and Italy. In the latter two, regional accents are not decisive, in France what matters is the address, if not of your home then of your school or your firm. And *meimon* (distinguished school or family) rather than accent also is an important element of the élite in Japan – with the difference that a *meimon gakkō* (distinguished school) is thinkable in provincial Japan but not in provincial France. I thought at the time that national solidarity in the fight against an enemy threatening England's, indeed Europe's existence might, at last, melt the two classes. It now turns out that things are worse because of acerbated industrial strife and the influx of poor immigrants from former colonies. There is now some *hangan-biiki*[33] (sympathy for the underdog) in my affection for England.

At any rate, the English were good to me at difficult times. Whether I acquired something of their pragmatic and basically tolerant world view I cannot say. But I came to admire them for it. It influenced my personal view of Christianity as a belief to show itself in action, more than in theory.

I also wish to state here that the literature of England, ever since I passed a few years in the country and later, in Tokyo, became a member of the English Literature Department of my university, has endeared itself to me more than any other of the literatures I have studied. By 'endear' I mean 'secure my affection', not 'command my admiration'. The *koine* of New Testament Greek can be so awkwardly simple as to bring tears to the eye. The Greek of Demosthenes or the Latin of Tacitus bring alive in a few artistically structured paragraphs a strange but majestic world. Both French and German literatures have climbed heights superior to English literature, but both have also fallen deeper than English ever has: rationalism has wrought havoc in France, sentimentalism in Germany. But of literature in the English language it must be said that it consistently appeals to mind and heart – it never becomes tiring, it rarely becomes irrelevant. I have always felt a peculiar attraction, since I am a born German, to the Germanic overtones of old English, such as *Beowulf,* and as still clearly audible in Chaucer, or even in Thomas More. But the uniqueness of English literature may he precisely in the fact that its writers managed to absorb, starting with Norman French, other languages into its vocabulary and structure, thus making poets, novelists and playwrights aware of the continuity within the changeability of language. It is the men of letters who have done it in every century. They have given the language an almost magical resilience and thus also made possible the miracle of contemporary American literature, the product of a different civilization but naturally in the English tradition. Shakespeare is the greatest European writer because he has masterfully displayed this spirit of adaptability and sure touch at the very moment when that little island stood at the verge of becoming the first world power of the new age.

If I may briefly speak of Japanese literature in this comparative context I confess to feelings such as Lafcadio Hearn[34] appears to have had. I do not think that Hearn knew Japanese to the point of mastering it. But he was poet enough to feel its beauty as a poet. He also was fond of the literature as expressing the soul of the national culture totally different from, if not opposed to, the European tradition. Hearn thought that in the monism of Herbert Spencer[35] a world view similar to Japan's was evolving in the West. This was a crude simplification. But there is a particle of truth with which I would agree. The language in its very structure corresponds much more with the scepticism and agnosticism of the Western world, as it becomes more modern and sophisticated. To Hearn – not a well-educated man – Spencer was a typical representative of that modern West. In reality, Spencer spoke for a doctrinaire and arrogant materialism almost the opposite of the Japanese spirit. Japan's spirit, as expressed in the language, is full of ambiguity, indications, suggestions, anacolutha, unfinished sentences, double or treble negatives. It often fails to clarify numbers, genders or tenses. It reveals moods more frequently than clear-cut statements. It is thus eminently adapted to express thinking from which certainty and absoluteness increasingly disappear. Modern man is either the victim of ideologues promising Utopia around the corner and ready for violence to actuate it. Or else he is diffident and unsure about absolutes, sceptical of certainties, except the certainty that there are rarely definite answers. Japanese literature as well as the Japanese language mirror this latter modern mood most adequately. Spencer, in contrast, is the ideologue, hence not really cognate with the Japanese temperament.

The *Haruna Maru* which I boarded in Liverpool in June 1940 was one of the last, if not the last, Japanese commercial ships to sail the dangerous waters around Europe. Slowly we sailed around the Cape of Good Hope, since the Suez Canal was closed, and wherever we entered a port, it was invariably a British possession and I, as an alien of an enemy country, had to remain aboard, watched by a British sentinel.

The passengers consisted of Englishmen on their way to the colonies, of the wives and children of Japanese diplomats in England, and of Japanese businessmen and intellectuals from France. *Haruna Maru* had waited in Lisbon several days for the arrival of the latter. With these I became good friends, especially the late Komatsu Kiyoshi who, after the war, introduced me as a member to the Japanese Pen Club.

For the Japanese ladies and their children I improvised courses in German and Latin. It was then that I came to admire the gift for languages and the zeal to learn which characterize Japanese women in apparent contrast to the men. I do not think, of course, that there are innate differences between the two sexes in regard to language. But in the same way that Japanese women, regardless of social status or regional provenience, speak a Japanese very easily understandable to us foreigners, so also do they pick up our languages much more readily. Is it the assiduity and dedication which a woman has to display if she wants to acquire or keep a position in this society? Perhaps it is not a purely Japanese phenomenon, due to the larger dispensation of *amae* (indulgence) to men, and consequently the stricter expectation of hard work from women.

Perhaps women in most societies speak in a more precise and conscientious fashion. At any rate, I have always found it easier to learn a foreign language from the ladies.

The tense international situation was completely omitted from conversation on board ship, as can be done among Japanese. The ship's daily bulletin also managed to leave out exciting news. We were never informed of the 'Battle of Britain' being won at the time by the Royal Air Force, nor that the second Konoe Cabinet was unable to bring the China Conflict to a halt.

When at last, in September, we reached Kobe, the first feeling to well up in me was gratitude. Only a short while ago in England it looked as if I would never be able to return. Indeed, the first English newspapers we saw in Lisbon, only dated late June, a few days after our departure, prominently displayed the news, 'all Germans in England put into camps'. (I later learned that they were eventually shipped to camps in Canada and Australia.) Three months later, here I was safely, back 'home'.

A second feeling overcame me. The people looked emaciated, clad in the poor material called *sufu* (staple fibre) (a word no longer intelligible to Japanese under fifty, I imagine), and little of that cheerfulness which had impressed me five years earlier upon arriving in Shimonoseki via Siberia. But even in their poverty, the people were noble and dignified. *Bushi wa kuwanedo* ... I thought, and felt a new wave of warmth for them. I soon discovered that information was scarce; no details seemed to be known about the European War.

A reporter for *Bungei Shunjū* (a monthly magazine) came up to me at Kobe port asking for an essay on 'England about to fall to Hitler'. Well, I had the feeling that England would not fall so easily. Furthermore, I had decided not to speak evil of a country that had been nice to me in perilous times. The reporter conceded I might write on another theme concerned with England in wartime. I wrote an essay about my agony of collecting twelve books out of my largish collection in London for my long voyage back. The essay was printed in *Bunshun* vol. – No. – (perhaps Oct. or Nov. or Dec. 1940). It was my first appearance in Japanese print.

Back in Tokyo, I discovered that the political turbulance of the times had reached Sophia University where I was beginning to teach that autumn. It was the time of *Shintaisei* (new system), a word I heard then for the first time. The then President, Fr Heuvers, had to resign as *gakuchō* (head of the university) – no foreigner throughout the whole country should be *chō* (chief) anymore. (I confess this regulation did not shock me and I still believe that – although there are exceptions – some such practice ought to prevail even now.) At any rate, Father Heuvers cheerfully obliged. I was impressed by his brief speech at a ceremony in the *kōdō* (assembly hall); indeed, few foreigners have served me until now as a better example of totally selfless devotion to the Japanese people.

Everything I had been toiling at for many years was now going to be put to the test. That was my feeling in these momentous days. My experience as priest and teacher, my knowledge of several classical and modern languages and literatures, and the solidarity I felt with the Japanese destiny.

As it turned out, I still had to serve a few more years of apprenticeship. There was, first of all, the unnatural atmosphere of the year preceding Pearl Harbor and then of the Pacific War. People often ask me whether I was maltreated in those hectic days. I definitely never was. I am still convinced that there was no real xenophobia in this country. There was much rather clumsy propaganda against the 'white devils': but it was barely believed in, even by the half-educated, although I have heard of a few rather barbaric acts against foreigners in the provinces. There was, however, as I came to understand much later, the reality of *dōshitsusei* (students in the same room) the instinctive group togetherness without saying much, let alone arguing. This time, the threatened group was not one village or one clan or one family, but the nation itself. In the beginning I was to feel annoyed when people studiously avoided asking me about the state of Europe or answering my questions on Japan, and all the things that had happened. By and by I came to understand that I was experiencing that most characteristic feature of Japanese behaviour, reticence. Indeed, much as totalitarianism, when rising, was noisily and persistently talked about in Europe but rarely mentioned in Japan, so now the war and the danger of war was met with silence here, while in England it was the unchanging centre of conversation. Words, to the Japanese, are not the only way to express one's feelings. Emotions can be so overwhelming that words can only mislead. '*Kokoro amarite kotoba tarazu,*'[37] (the heart is full words are lacking) says Ki no Tsurayuki about Ariwara no Narihira. There is something deeply attractive about this ascetical or abstemious, – I would like to say – attitude to language. But it postulates an effort, until the foreigner grasps it.

The times, during which the inhabitants of the Japanese archipelago slowly and, so it seemed, inevitably slid into the War, were not filled by intolerant chauvinism, but they were not times of cosmopolitanism either. Yet, the study of comparative culture and literature, let alone of a universal religion flourishes the better, the larger the intellectual horizon of the *Zeitgeist* (spirit of the time). During my first years as a professor, the horizon was narrowed down from above, by censorship, poverty and, as the war progressed, sheer despair. At Jōchi Daigaku (Sophia University), certain difficulties were especially noticeable which had arisen a few years before I first came. At the height of the *Manshū Jiken* (Manchurian Incident), some of our students had refused to bow in reverence to the enshrined souls at Yasukuni shrine – without, it must be stressed, any instigation on the part of their teachers, let alone the foreign

Fathers. The uproar in military and right-wing circles as well as the press was frightening, and as one of the various resulting pressures, applications went down rapidly and a particularly unsavory *haizoku shōkō* (military officers attached to a school) became attached to the university.

When I began to teach, we were hardly known in the country except for this 'Yasukuni incident', and our students were woefully few. There was no curriculum in those days to include lectures on acculturation, cultural intercourse or comparative literature. For a few years, in effect, I did little more than teach languages.

Teaching languages is, indeed, the best way to become friends with students, since one gets to know them. My senior German colleagues on the staff had all arrived with doctorates from the best universities abroad: Cambridge, Columbia, Munich, Berlin, Zürich, Köln (Cologne). They were eagerly lecturing in their respective fields, but felt frequently frustrated. They could not convey their ideas, because of their own ignorance of Japanese and their students' inadequate knowledge of foreign languages. I remember one colleague remarking to me: 'Each time I leave the classroom, I feel like a drenched poodle.' The poodle feels particularly uncomfortable when leaving the water, and so a foreigner in a class of yawning or half-asleep students unable to follow the professors' line of thought. To teach a language is definitely simple in comparison, as also the teaching of a foreign literature if it consists in reading text. But the real goal of the dedicated university professor goes further than teaching a language for its own sake. He is then up to the immense difficulty of how to express himself in a language he has spent years learning and has never properly mastered. Fortunately, in those early days I was not sufficiently aware of what was to remain a problem of my own, even if to a lesser extent – given the opportunities I had had to study Japanese – than many of my friends and colleagues.

My teaching load was light and became increasingly lighter;

once the Pacific War broke out students finally began to be called into the army. My students then were not necessarily the brightest graduates of the best middle schools, but I have rarely again had the pleasure I then experienced: students with the first buds of intellectual curiosity barely opening but then, by dint of much individual attention and plenty of study, suddenly blooming. Some have remained my friends for life.

I was young and restless, had time on my hands, and was therefore glad to be offered the direction of an intellectual circle for friends interested in Catholicism. The circle, called *Kulturheim*, (literally culture home) had been founded by Fr Bitter and then mostly had been the work of Takemiya Hayato who had later left in order to set up *Rokkōgakuen* (school) in Kobe. The circle met once a month or so. It was located in a splendid, half-timbered mansion built in the latter part of Meiji period by what must have been an opulent general of the Imperial Army. The club-rooms where we met, as well as the upper floor providing a quiet chapel looking out into the garden, have meanwhile been completely refurbished. By now, the whole house has come to be called *Kulturheim*, not a German word at all, but one of those *kokusan gairaigo* (Japanese-created foreign word) like *sararyman* (salary-man) or *O.L.* (office lady). Indeed, the house is so popular among students for weddings that *Kulturheim* is occasionally mentioned as the name of a Church, 'St *Kulturheim Kyōkai*'.

Here my first diffident steps in Japanese took place; the painful introductions of a speaker or the halting words of thanks. The small audience of students and colleagues from various universities and other intellectuals – seldom more than about fifty – assembled in a very friendly and appreciative mood.

I try in these reminiscences, to speak as little as possible of people still alive and active. Otherwise I could enumerate a considerable number of great and wonderful people young and old – come to listen or to help – who in the post-war years established their name in learning, teaching, administration the media; some of them now priests and nuns, many of them parents and grandparents – occasionally their offsprings coming to see me. It was a heart-warming time for cultural interaction on the personal plane, when nothing except war seemed to be possible between nations. And we kept on meeting till bombs began to fall on Tokyo.

There was a brief air attack on Tokyo in November 1944; I remember trying to be humorous and using the term *otoshidama* (New Year gift) for the bombs at the regular November meeting. Later, a young man came up to me and reprimanded me for making such a frivolous remark in a national hour of need. I do not easily take to heart such remarks; on the contrary, I am inclined to accept amendments cheerfully as a man 'from the outside' should. But I remember being hurt then, because the young speaker appeared totally impervious to my good intentions. I will admit here, that humour is indeed the hardest element of one country to be exported into another, as I have once described in an address to the *Nihon Eibun Gakkai* (Japan English literary association) published in *Eibungatea to Eigogaton* (1979). Few jokes can be properly translated, and the attempt may result in a new joke. The only fear I have, when trying to be humorous in Japanese, is to be misunderstood as sarcastic. Before I found this out, I may have offended many people without knowing it. The fact that sarcasm and irony are disliked in this country is another proof of its degree of civilization. In a humane culture confrontations should be avoided, and sarcasm is a public reproof, effected by what the speaker imagines as his superior wit, in other words it is *meiwaku* (trouble) produced by haughtiness. The element of morality enters here, as so often, into the realm of cultural encounter. At the same time I still feel that the young Japanese critic should have known me enough to forgive my remark.

The name of another young man who frequented our meetings I can reveal, because he is no longer alive: Noguchi

contact with him and helped to win contributors and sub-scribers. Upon my returning in 1940 I joined the editorial committee and was soon appointed acting editor.

The quarterly had already then established an international reputation as the only scholarly review dedicated exclusively to Japan. Fr Kraus who knew little Japanese had a remarkable talent for collecting people and fascinating them with his projects. Young as I still was, I felt proud to be able to put my knowledge of languages and literatures at the disposal of the journal. Articles and reviews were accepted in English, French and German. I at once introduced the custom of summarizing all articles in both English and Japanese. The few years that followed were happy and intense, but they were short. Soon, in December of the year I had returned from England, the Pacific War broke out and as it neared its end, *Monumenta Nipponica* gave up the ghost. It reappeared again six years after the defeat and is at present run exclusively in English by one of my English Jesuit brethren.

From 1940 to 1944, much of my time and energy was devoted to the quarterly. With the increasing militarist temper and the thorough cut-off from warring Europe, a spirit of isolation was in the air. I feel grateful now for the unique opportunity of delving deeply into the Japanese past.

Much of my work consisted of keeping in touch with contributors, soliciting manuscripts, reading proofs, and remaining in touch with the printers. I remember a visit made to Prof. Shidehara Michitarō to discuss the next instalment of his *Zeami Kadensho* translation instalment. I rang the door-bell at the house near Sendagaya Station: an elderly gentleman in kimono came to the door. I took him for some old-fashioned butler. But it was his father himself, former foreign minister Shidehara Kijūrō.[43] We had a friendly chat. He remembered me three years later when, for a short time, he became Prime Minister.

Much of my work consisted in overhauling translations of work submitted to the editor by Japanese scholars and in adding explanatory notes. Such articles were, for example, extracts from *Taiheiki*[44] concerning *Dainankō*.[45] The story impressed me as that of a military hero interested as much in trickery as in valour, and in cleverly escaping as much as in murderous battle, a very humane warrior, loyal to the *Tenno* (Emperor) in a saner manner than the shrill slogans of the militarists in my time would suggest. *Rangaku Kotohajime*[46] was to me an even more fascinating discovery: Sugita Gempaku[47] and his friends groping their way through an unfathomable language, without linguistic help, while escaping the harassment of the *Bakufu* police in order to learn the secrets of the human anatomy – that is to me one of the more dramatic manifestations of the Japanese spirit of inquiry, passionate and patient alike. One more translation effort I like to remember is Yanagi Sōetsu's[48] *Mokujiki Shōnin*, an illuminating portrayal of the wandering bonze who left his carved and painted pieces of folk art to comfort the common people of the Edo period while himself leading the life of an aesthete. I found the *tanka* (short poems), he composed for all manner of occasions, extensively quoted by Mr Yanagi, especially rewarding. Against the tendency in European Christianity to overemphasize logical consistency, *Mokujiki Shōnin* stands for a heart-warming, all-encompassing religion, a synthesis of generosity and compassion. Yanagi Sōetsu had written this valuable contribution for our journal. My Sunday visits to his house in Komaba, where I met many of his friends and collaborators, such as Hamada Shoji,[48] belong to my most cherished memories of the war years. He was also a valued speaker at the *Kulturheim*. His wife, the great soprano, graced our Christmas party with her songs.

The final work of Japanese studies I accomplished during the war was an analysis of Shimazaki Tōson as a novelist. I wrote my study originally in German for a *Festschrift* in honour of some jubilee of the German Cultural Institute in Kyoto. But the German defeat prevented publication. I rewrote the piece in English, and it appeared in *Monumenta Nipponica* after the war. Tōson had been living in Banchō, just across from our house in Kioichō. Although I never met him, it was on the advice of his *monkasei* (disciples) such as Oda Masanobu and Yanagiya Takeo that I began to read his book.

None of it had been translated into English. Meanwhile, several translations have appeared and I was asked to contribute to the entry on him for *Encyclopedia Britannica*, 1970. There I wrote that he did much 'through his fiction to illuminate the clash of old and new forces in a Japan feverishly modernizing itself, and the unsettling effect of this collision on the intellectual'.

I cannot say whether such studies contributed much to Japanology; they certainly deepened my attachment to Japan. My views about this nation had roots deep enough to make me ignore the temporary aberrations in the cultural climate of the war years and the years immediately after. The works I studied cover over a thousand years from Heian to Shōwa, starting with *Ise Monogatari* and ending with Tōson. They touch on very different aspects of the Japanese soul, but radiate the same common denominator: feeling of unity with nature and distrust of ideology. These studies confirmed my earliest impressions of Japan. They also made me suspicious of the panaceas which, in abundance, were offered alike from outside and within, once the war was over.

When we all emerged, from our ruined houses – I had spent the entire war in the midst of Tokyo, in rags and underfed – I was not one of those many despairing of Japan's future. Nor did I subscribe to any of the wonder drugs then offered to Japan. I fervently believed in her continuity as an individual entity between the cultures. I was also firmly convinced that she would never relapse into cultural isolationism.

CHAPTER FOUR

Cultural Interaction

 —————— oOo ——————

This is a record of a life's *kenkyū* (research, study) – not of a life. But the study of comparative culture comes nearer to one's personal life than most research. Much is involved: not only the study of Western civilization as compared with that of Japan, but also that of a priest living in a secularized society.

In other words, if I am to describe my studies, I have to describe myself. Both West and East, both religious and secular worlds are the subject-matter of myself as well as my study. I will, therefore, have to stick to a few principal points to trace outlines. The comparison of various cultures had, throughout the years of my formation, opened my horizon and shaped my ego. How did it show in the teaching, writing and guiding of my subsequent years?

When the war ended, I found myself with a few Japanese and German companions in the buildings, partly burnt-out but partly intact, of Kōjimachi (Kōjimanchi is near the British Embassy and the Imperial palace) where I had been living since my first arrival in 1935 and, in fact, am living still. Everything was in ruins. One five-storey building remained, the present *ichigōkan* (number/building), at the time one of the few of its size between Shinjuku and Ginza, between Kanda and Shimbashi.

Our feelings soon after listening to the 'diamond sound' (declaration of surrender by the Emperor) were of rather black despair. I was convinced that the Allies would turn Japan into a poor farmers' republic much as Baruch Morgenthau had advocated doing with Germany. Fortunately, as soon as the Americans landed, they began to act differently, often clumsily, but always benevolently. At the same time, our Japanese friends who had been so stunned as to be speechless, slowly recovered their courage. I have often been asked to state what were my happiest moments in Japan. There have been so many, I find it difficult to decide. But surely one of those moments was to discover that October, among the ruins at Sukiyabashi, a street-vendor displaying frying pans made of bomb splinters. So fast had they begun to recover.

The ingeniously produced frying pan was only an outward symbol of a process of rebirth. The people were not only physically rising from the ashes. They were also spiritually overcoming the hysterical narrowness of the unhappy seclusion. *Sakoku* (isolation) has always had to be imposed upon the national mind. It has never been a natural condition. As old friends now came to look me up again and the students of my and of other universities flocked back to their *sensei*, I came to feel acutely the need to put cultural comparisons into action. Prompted by my friends I began to write about the background ideas of my own culture – not to proselytize but to point to the *yōkon* (Western spirit). *Wakon yōsai* (Japanese spirit Western learning) had been the slogan of the Meiji enlightenment. The dark hour of the present called for a deeper research.

I began to write, under some stress, I admit. I was so emaciated from hunger, that my mother in Germany broke down in tears when she saw my photograph. I was unable in those days to correspond, but an American chaplain I had known in Tokyo managed to look her up in Germany.

My first booklet was entitled Elements of Logic (*Ronrigaku Yōsetsu*). This was based on lectures I had delivered at *Seishin Joshi Senmon* (Sacred Heart Women's School) during the war when all the English and American nuns had been interned. I still have vivid memories of the girls in my classes. They managed to look smart even in their *monpei* (kind of bloomers) and they were assiduous students, although they may not have cared much for logic. The Japanese public did certainly not care much for my book ..., the first publication of Enderle Shoten after the war. I still think that such a title, in the midst of despair, was somewhat funny. But it was well meant: an appeal to reason after the disasters of an irrational war. But Aristotelean logic does not appeal to most Japanese in search of common sense. I have long come to understand that they think existentially. '*Le coeur a des raisons que la Raison ne connaît point*': this saying by Pascal is more in the line with their thinking.

I wrote three further books during this period, in an endeavour to facilitate an encounter with the West on a deeper level than the ephemeral, I hope demonstrating a greater understanding of their needs. *Christokyō to Kindai Bunka* (Christianity and contemporary culture) and *Catholicism* appeared in the series *Atene Bunko* selling at ¥20 per copy, with narrow print and on wartime paper. The small, high-brow booklets brought letters and visits by dozens of young men. Even now I keep running into middle-aged men, students of *shūsen chokugo* (immediately after the end of the war), who show me their yellowed copies of the booklets now to be had in second-hand bookshops only with difficulty. Or again students will show me their father's copy of years ago. I may get around to rewrite them – then in their complicated *kanji* (characters) and *okurigana* (kana written alongside a Chinese character to show its Japanese reading) – for a modern edition.

But I feel also they ought to be left as they are as a nostalgic monument to cultural intercourse in arduous times. The present needs different things.

The third publication of those days appeared in the Shinshō series of the same publisher, Kōbundō, *Yōroppa no Kiki* (Europe's crisis). It was a labour of love – my first critical analysis of the ideas of freedom, equality and progress as they had taken shape in the democratic philosophy, especially of the Anglo-Americans. It is perhaps the only time I came near to formulating a philosophy of comparative culture in the modern world, and some of my friends consider the book a prophetic warning against certain excesses of Euro-American democracy that have, since, become acute in Japan itself. However, thirty years ago, the times were not ripe for such warnings to be accepted. The book was only a moderate success, and in addition the publishing house Kōbundō went out of business.

Besides writing for the general public, I also made efforts, with my collaborators, to extend the small *Kulturheim* circle to a larger audience. We organized *Kōkai Kōza* (public lectures) in the University Hall. We had Yoshikawa Eiji[50] (novelist), or Hasegawa Nyozekan[51] (Asahi journalist) and suchlike famous writers for an occasional symposium with one or the other of our European Fathers or American friends. The late Fr Candau was, in due time, one of our most effective speakers. Indeed, what little I myself have learned by way of public speaking in Japanese, I have learned from him. The pity is, I did not have quite his genius for mixing a stirring style with a thought-provoking message and an occasional humorous interruption. People were listening to him with rapt attention. He needed this kind of enthusiastic audience to deliver his best. But it would be mistaken to imagine that he only improvised on the spur of the moment. He carefully polished his manuscript, learned it more or less by heart, occasionally even practising in front of a mirror. He also had systematically studied the structure of the Japanese psyche, long before the *Nihonjinron* (theory of Japaneseness) of our days had become the fashion. After his death I wrote an article on the secret of this great personality in *The Missionary Bulletin* Vol. 10, No. 3, 1955.

The lectures for large audiences, however, were less important in our programme than survey courses on literature, philosophy, theology and the like. Theology proved extraordinarily attractive. We soon had to arrange a two-year curriculum for all branches of theology, such as dogmatics, morals, church history, canon law – and these courses are still continuing. The university courses for *shakaijin* (members of society) now flourishing at Sophia University, recognized a few years ago as 'Community College,' have their seeds in our post-war efforts. Outwardly, the venture is not so different from the culture lectures now arranged for the public at various places. But I think that the inner spirit of post-war foundation-time – the bringing together of people from both inside and outside Japan – still characterizes the present programme with its many non-Japanese teachers, classes in a great variety of languages, and even non-Japanese students. In those days dozens of American and British officers, soldiers and seamen would teach conversation and translation, and a tradition of fraternization began which has not been interrupted since.

The English language sector of the *Kōkai Kōza* (public lectures) which I had started with little more than cheerful enthusiasm and a number of devoted friends led, very soon, to a most vigorous new growth. When the late American Fr A. Miller joined us in the early 1950s, I asked him for his help. Having had useful academic experience in the US and great organizational talent, he soon built up the International Division of the University into a Department which came to be recognized by the US University Federation and further developed it until it is now a *Mombushō* (Ministry of Education)-recognized department, teaching all subjects in English and providing Japanese degrees.

These hectic post-war years remain with me as an indelible memory of cultural intercourse on the human level. The assiduity of hundreds of Japanese, old and young, to inquire into knowledge, taboo until yesterday, reminded me of St Francis Xavier's[52] first impression of the Japanese as 'full of intellectual curiosity'.

A similar phenomenon simultaneously developed among the Americans in evening classes together with English-speaking Japanese and other Asians. I was put in charge of a lecture on Japanese Cultural History. I taught it, principally with the help of George Sansom's[53] books, for about a dozen years. To me there was nothing startling in the quickness of perception and delicacy of feeling the Japanese showed in matters of an alien culture. But I had not thought that young Americans would take so seriously to the subtle nuances of the cultural background of Japan. To tell the truth, while I was conversant enough with various European ways of life, I had never known Americans to speak of, and it took me some time even to get used to their accent. The admirable thing, at any rate, was to have, among others, students of the victorious army meekly and happily studying the culture of their defeated enemy. Here they were, till late into the night, listening, learning their lessons, submitting their papers and also providing pleasant debates. Happily, the colloquy has continued. In the few decades since the War, English, Australian, but specially American scholars have contributed more to an understanding of Japan than all foreign scholars since before the Meiji Restoration. Some are my *kōhai* (juniors) from London, my *deshi* (disciples) from Tokyo, others respected friends. Of everyone I am proud, as I am of my Japanese students, especially of those days. The privileged young today have no idea of the handicap of war and post-war times when anybody reading a book in English in public risked having it kicked out of his hands. Nor do they know how hard it was to find English books to read when the war was over. There was, in those days,

shortage of everything. But there was an abundance of enthusiasm, and the study of an alien culture flourishes best where
there is plenty of enthusiasm.

Meanwhile, my principal occupation, teaching Japanese students in the university proper, had once again begun to take
most of my time. As the boys came back from the war and new
young men enrolled, the onus of lectures increased. Most of my
work in Japan has consisted in teaching Japanese students in
the classroom. I have taught English literature and
Comparative Literature, European Intellectual History, English
Composition, Reading, Speaking, German and French through
the medium of English. Whether I was a good teacher or not,
I cannot say. At any rate, I have always taught with zest. I was
also always animated by a motive very pure in itself: I always
felt the obligation of *ongaeshi* (returning an obligation).
Teachers of various countries – including Japan, from my days
in London on – had taught me the knack of discovering a new
fruit, patiently open it and slowly, carefully relish its taste. It
was this skill I wanted to teach my students, and thus repay a
debt to my own international body of teachers. With this is
connected my perpetual endeavour to bring in bits of etymol-
ogy in order to place the language back into its cultural context.

If I were to count my teaching work in hours of time spent,
I would probably have to admit that it was teaching foreign languages to Japanese. I have read texts with them, both slowly
and at a rapid clip. I have lectured to them in English, but I
admit usually with brief escapades in Japanese. I have corrected
their translations (and it often cost me almost an hour to deal
with four or five pages). 1 have read their essays, both in
English and Japanese. The former are often very neatly done,
but by and large they are boring, because they are repetitive and
are too limited because of the small vocabulary of the student.
Essays in Japanese concerning a lecture heard, books read or
just reflections, are, on the other hand, invariably fascinating. I
wish Xerox would then have been as universally available as it

is now. I would by now have a collection of truly acute insights into alien worlds by Japanese youngsters. The Japanese are gifted with great perception, and the Japanese language, if handled with love, is a beautiful instrument to produce a mood and to evoke nostalgia.

I do not believe that the Japanese as a nation do not have a gift for languages. They are not rash and impetuous but decorous and cautious. Performance must be preceded by rehearsal. Spontaneity is frowned upon. Hence they are reluctant to voice their opinions, for fear of hurting somebody's feelings or losing face. That can be a handicap on the international level, but it is offset by the confidence which the Japanese inspire through their conscientious and meticulous thoroughness. Volubility is not necessarily proof of sincerity.

There are many complaints nowadays that something must be wrong with foreign language training in Japan, considering the few English-speaking people among the millions who have studied compulsory English before they go to college and while they are at college. I am not enough of an expert to make unchallengeable statements in these matters. Frankly speaking, however, I consider the present method of learning English superior to an education which puts the emphasis on speaking rather than reading, writing and hearing. Native English speakers find that the Japanese study English grammar and syntax too assiduously. But they forget that the Japanese do not want to learn any of the simplified variants such as those spoken by ex-colonial people. They also have the sound instinct that a foreign language must not be studied so one-sidedly that one's own is forgotten.

Critics of Japanese foreign language learning also forget that English is one of the hardest languages in the West. English is easy for the beginner to express simple things, and that is the greatest attraction of English. But English has the largest vocabulary of any Western language, and it has hardly any universal rules of sentence structure and pronunciation. The Japanese as a nation are by temperament serious; they have never been colonialized; and they want to know the reasons for what they are doing. Personally, I would strongly advocate, in the interest of cultural interchange, that they continue teaching the language from early on in life, step by step. Thus a splendid training of the mind will be provided, the doors opened to a strange world, and the foundation laid for speaking when the challenge arises. Short courses can teach the individual enough to converse with foreigners, such as a taxi driver, a page boy, a steward, a hostess, a sales girl. Academics need longer. At any rate, while English speaking should not be totally omitted from the English curriculum, speech should not be the main, let alone the only purpose. To speak a language even moderately well, a certain gift of mimicry as well as a musical ear is needed. Not everybody has this; it would be unfair to judge all by the same yardstick.

Interest in language has grown immensely in recent years. That has certainly to do with rapidly shrinking distances of communication in our world. Computers and satellites are taking over. And as a scientific method of language 'linguistics', has arisen. This new science omits such 'non-scientific' considerations as tradition, harmony and beauty. It prefers abstract mathematical and statistic formulas. Language becomes divorced from its living context, especially the context of literature. The study of language is no longer 'normative' but 'descriptive'. It is undeniable that thanks to this method new insights into the inner structure of languages have been obtained. It is also true that simplification helps the illiterate and foreigners. But the disregard for norms in teaching a given language can become disastrous. Professors of linguistics have formed powerful *batsu* (groups/factions) at the universities in various countries for example, West Germany, and now, in effect, control the curricula of primary and secondary schools. It is shameful to sacrifice rules and tradition for the sake of convenience. A living language in all its complexity should be esteemed as a treasure house. And that is true of one's own as well as a foreign language. To come to love a language is to learn it truly, i.e. making it one's own. And a fitting way to learn to love it is to look for it in literature.

All this sounds very unrealistic, I admit, since few Japanese have the opportunity to put their knowledge of foreign languages to use. But the practical point of view never ought to be the only one. Furthermore, to acquire skills while young is a marvellous investment for the whole life. The faculty of memory begins to lose acumen after a man's twenties, but man retains for always what he has acquired when young. This is also true of a second or third language and, at the risk of repeating myself, I wish to state that the best way for a Japanese to learn, say, French or German or Russian is to do it through English.

The teaching of a foreign language on the college level can be turned into an exercise of teaching a foreign culture. That is what I have tried to do, whether successfully or not, in my language and literature classes. Still, I have also valiantly tried to teach my own specialty in the classroom. That is no easy thing for the non-Japanese professor. He is usually expected to use a foreign language, and I respect this wish in a country where encounters with a foreigner are so few. What I did do, usually ended up in the same way. I began by using English, after a while the students' attention started to flag and I found myself talking more slowly and even repeating myself. The result would be that some of the students, often the best ones, were falling asleep from boredom. I would finally switch to Japanese to sum up the principal points of my lecture.

Among colleagues we would occasionally discuss possible answers to the common problem: how to use a foreign language to young people without putting them to sleep. I remember one colleague insisting that he had no such problem: everybody, he said, was so fascinated by his way of talking that some students even put on a hearing-aid to follow better. Such can be the professor's self-delusion. The fact was, and everybody knew, that his students were using not a hearing-aid but a transistor radio to while away the time listening to a baseball match or some jazz.

In the more than thirty years since the end of the war, the level of English language understanding has increased spectacularly, certainly at my university. But until recently I have found it necessary to revivify the audience by a brief summary in Japanese, plus a humerous story or so. In addition, I soon discovered that one must pay attention to the mood of the listening students. Certainly that is true of girl students. The American essayist and lexicographer Henry L. Mencken has observed: 'A man's womenfolk, whatever their show of respect for his merit and authority, always regard him secretly as an ass, and with something akin to pity.' He speaks of America, but his observation applies well to Europe and best to Japan. They apply not only to women in the family, but also in the classroom. I only want to add one other thing: women must *like* a professor, in order to listen to him attentively and cooperate. I am not sure, but I think they dislike pomposity, narrow-mindedness and irascibility. The latter, I am afraid, has from time to time made me sound *kowai* (frightening). But by and large they have responded well to me. I am grateful to countless nods of approval and smiles of understanding during lectures, the faultless reports and exams, the friendly greetings on streets and *densha* (trains or electric trams). I also wish to state my ardent wish that the groves of academe in Japan be more widely opened to women as lecturers and professors. The field of linguistic communication, particularly through literature, would benefit immensely from a more active contribution by women.

As for male students, comparatively few high-school boys nowadays select the *bungakubu* (literature department) for further studies, and that is also largely the case in Europe and America. It is quite conceivable that the *bungakubu* is thought of as raising future teachers, and that the teaching profession is coming to be increasingly the domain of women. That may be a good thing; at any rate, the atmosphere in lectures and literature seminars is acquiring an element of cheer and joy which helps the appreciation of literature in the usually so decorous air of this country. Male students profit from a welcome absence of inhibition. But, I have dicsovered in these years that masculine precision and analytic power remains fortunately intact. Also, the comparative method suits the masculine mind.

Instead of generalizing, may I be allowed briefly to sketch the portrait of one male student of mine, typical of many of my students, but also unique in the heroic proportion of his virtues. He died and so I may mention his name: Yamaguchi Seiji. When he died, he had barely become *kōshi* (lecturer) at our university. I wrote this about him in 'English Literature and Language':

> When I occasionally ask myself whether it is really meaningful to have spent the greater part of my life in this country, the memory of Yamaguchi Seiji comes to my mind reassuringly. There are many friends of mine like him, some still alive, some no longer among us, who represent to me the kind of humaneness I would perhaps never have encountered except in Japan. But the self-effacing yet straightforward personality of Yamaguchi made me realize a particularly attractive blend of Japanese characteristics.
>
> I first came to know him when he joined our graduate school, where he completed both the Master's and the Doctor's course. He was already an all-round, mature person, having finished his undergraduate studies while fending for himself during the arduous post-war days and having saved the money to pay for his postgraduate studies while working for a time in the library of the British Council.
>
> As a student he struck me as a man capable both of delving into a difficult specialty – in his case, the minor playwrights of the Elizabethan age – and of ranging farther afield, not only into other periods and genres of English literature but also into

the general intellectual background of English and European letters. The first preoccupation led to his scholarly dissertation, the other to his unfailingly interesting performance as a teacher and a contributor to the quarterly *Sophia*, as well as, finally, to his conversion to Christianity.

His numerous contributions to our quarterly cover an amazing variety of subjects, from the medieval mystery plays to the tradition of the Shakespearean sonnet and More and Erasmus – to the point of fastidiousness. I remember a review of Alvin Kernan's book on the Renaissance in England entitled *The Cankered Muse*. It took him some research and ingenuity until he hit upon the word *dokuzetsu* as a translation of *cankered*, thus felicitously rendering the slightly malicious wit of the phrase. The meticulously written manuscripts themselves – a veritable joy to an editor – were a further proof of his conscientiousness.

I quote all this in full, because Yamaguchi in his whole attitude can serve as an example of many of my former students. I think he brought me to a deeper understanding of my own Christianity by joining my Sunday morning Bible sessions; he is one of the many who joined my faith, but at the same time applied a softening, warm and open touch to my religious convictions. Equally important is that he was typical of many of his fellow students by enlarging his horizon and looking beyond the subject of his doctoral thesis, as his early publications show.

I do not want to elaborate here on one important point. It is my conviction that the study of comparative literature postulates a certain moral fibre. Comparative literature needs both attachment and impartiality; otherwise it is not scientific. And these two do not easily co-exist, except in self-restrained, *enman na* (perfectionist) people such as Yamaguchi. During the ten years he stayed in the boarding house in Kazinokizaka the price for a cup of coffee went up from ¥20 to ¥200, his landlady never once raised her rent; the old lady was happy to have so reliable a man around.

As I grew older I came to prefer my work in the post-graduate school to that of the faculty. One reason is that I became personally involved at an early stage in establishing after the war the graduate school system at our university and of giving comparative culture and literature a vital role in it. But another reason may have been my mounting dislike of a new type of undergraduate student. The *shinsei* (new style)-system, introduced after the war, was to have widened the avenues to university study, and that was praiseworthy, and up to a point successful. But on the other hand, the reforms have also introduced abuses. When I came first to Japan, entrance examinations were not quite the hell they are now, and life after entrance was not quite so irresponsible as it now frequently is. The modern undergraduate can be very calculating in working out the minimum hours needed and in flattering his professors for the best marks. Little inner interest for his subject remains, especially when compared with his pastime pursuits and his career ambitions. Why the extra effort for a second language or a larger vision? He will say, Japanese society is harsh. The transition to total modernity is still in full swing. And perhaps the contemporary undergraduate is not so much the creator – the *chōhonnin* (ringleader) – of this condition as rather its victim. Perhaps a certain amount of anarchy in the undergraduate department is needed to compensate for the excessive rigour of the preceding school years as well as for the ensuing time of strictly regulated 'salaryman' life. The undergraduate is, at any rate, up against terrible odds. It is almost miraculous that in a general atmosphere of ease and relaxation, not to say of circus, so much serious response can so often be elicited. And that has been especially true of *Eibungakka* (English literature studies) among all *gakka* (subjects). I think back with gratitude on the common reading of Shakespeare dramas, Hegel texts, Eliot poems and contemporary political essays – where we grew into one community.

Apart from lectures on such themes as Literature and

Society, Modernity in Literature and the like, I used to hold a two-semester lecture *Yōroppa Bungaku Shisōshi* (History of thought in European culture). It was to be a really serious effort to introduce comparative literature on the undergraduate level. But it was not easy to make it accessible to all sections because of scheduling difficulties among the various sections.

Nor was the attempt to teach German and French as a second foreign language through the medium of English quite to succeed. I made the attempt twice, but neither lasted long despite many enthusiastic followers. The hours could not easily be fitted into the curriculum of other departments, I was told. Principally, however, the interest in the method was not as burning as I had thought. More energy on the part of both student and professor is expected than is readily given for so 'unimportant' a subject.

At any rate, those who kept attending my 'second-language-through-English' classes have been grateful, apart from becoming proficient. And as for my *bungaku-shisōshi* (history of thought in culture) I cherish one memory especially: the essays many students wrote with admirable dedication on a comparative topic of their choice, any two writers, books, periods or movements of two different national cultures.

It was in the graduate division that I was able to enlarge the comparative approach with more conviction. The idea of comparative literature as I see it I have expounded in *Sophia* vol. 2, no. 2. In contrast to the so-called 'Sorbonne Method' according to which only mutual influences in European Literature since the Renaissance can properly become the subject of comparative literature, I have followed a more widely admitted and more embracing definition. Not only influences on each other but also dependencies on common sources and archetypes, indeed, not only dependencies but meaningful similarities of style or matter can be the stuff of comparative literature, as can the contrasting treatment of a similar topic. The comparison must preferably be between authors of different languages.

This view is influenced by the philosophy of Herder, and by the great scholarly critics admired by my generation: Curtius, Auerbach and Hazard.

The subjects I have taken up in my graduate lectures and seminars were the tragic, the comic, religion and literature, politics and the novel, 'serious realism' in Western Literature etc. On the latter I lectured for the longest time. This lecture was principally based on Auerbach's *Mimesis* originally written in German, but meanwhile available also in English and Japanese translations. Auerbach, a German Jew, was famous as an expert of Romanist literature when he had to flee Hitler's persecution. He passed the war in Istanbul, far from his books, and produced his masterpiece which is, in effect, a survey of two millennia of European literature in the form of the interpretation of some twenty-five texts, from the Old Testament and Homer to Proust and Virginia Woolf. 'Mimesis', i.e., 'imitation', means the Platonic concept of mirroring reality in literature and art (*bungei*). It is assumed that those aspects of reality are depicted which are taken seriously, and it is further assumed that that which is 'becoming' will be considered worthier of attention than that which 'is', the dynamic rather than the static. These are the assumptions of historicism to which Auerbach subscribes. I have analysed this philosophy as it underlies Auerbach's major works – the first such attempt, I believe, ever made in Japan (*Sophia* vol. 16, no. 4). There are weaknesses in Auerbach's view of literature. His dislike for everything static, established and orderly and his fascination for the 'lowly,' i.e., what is oppressed, yet emerging, hence dynamic – Greco-Roman, Renaissance, or French classicism versus the Old and New Testament, Medieval chronicles and romances, French Realism and the Modern Stream of Consciousness – can be somewhat biased. But few books are more helpful to lead to an understanding of the *Zeitgeist* of various epochs and hence of ideas flowing through the centuries. For me, the highlights of the Seminar were the exposés of the participants, often in the shape of discussion, applying Auerbach's method to an author of their own field – from *Beowulf* to Saul Bellow.

I have always felt the urge to hold forth about things I had discovered, and to share my knowledge, old or new. It has remained my passion as a university professor as well as a religious believer. I do not claim that this is necessarily a pleasant trait. My mother used to say when, still a student, I would explain a point with raised forefinger: '*Jawohl, Herr Magister*' (which one might translate as '*Hai, sensei*' – 'Yes, master'). She had a lively sense of humour until she died, in 1978, at the age of ninety-seven. There was also a little irony in her using the word *sensei* to one too young for the title. When this desire to communicate is legitimized by learning and experience, then it can help to make lectures more interesting and publications more readable, since it is better to teach from a feeling of pleasure than a sense of duty. I cannot say that I have always succeeded. But I have always tried to avoid seeing only trees and no forest; to keep the vision wide open and not stay confined to one national literature, or one century of its history, or one writer, or one book. I do not deny the legitimacy of a solid, specialistic approach. But it does not seem to fit comparative literature as well as other branches of learning.

From the time we began preparing a graduate school in 1947 – as one of the first private universities and before any public one appeared – our thoughts began to converge on establishing an academic journal through which our university could best contribute to a Japan emerging from the ashes of the war, a Japanese equivalent to *Monumenta Nipponica*, i.e., a journal concerned with common problems of Western civilization as an entity, as *Monumenta Nipponica* was concerned with Japan as an entity. We were still an infinitesimally small college of only two *gakubu* (faculties), Letters and Economics, and it was comparatively easy to establish a consensus among the staff. I was asked to work out a plan.

The first issue of *Sophia, Seiyō Bunka narabi ni Tōzai Bunka*

Koryū no Kenkyū (study of Western culture and of the interchange between Eastern and Western cultures) appeared in 1952. It has been continuously published for more than thirty years, and I have been representing the editorial board most of the time, until my recent retirement. With none of my various activities in Japan have I identified myself as much as with this journal. Yet, if it has had any impact, that is due entirely to my collaborators, all colleagues of mine. There are more contributors, translators and advisers etc. than I could mention, even if I had not undertaken to name here only those no longer alive. The journal carried studies in comparative literature from the beginning, but it was principally interested in comparative culture, the 'cultural interaction between East and West' which characterized it from the beginning. It was to that theme that such leading scholars in the early years as Orui Noboru, Honjō Eijirō and Tsuji Zennosuke contributed. Inatomi Eijirō especially must be mentioned here as the great helper and inspirer. Despite his sad face of a Don Quixote he was yet a cheerful, indefatigable friend. He also had just the inner feeling for the comparative approach we needed. At any rate, he held that the Japanese should never lose sight of the European whole when tackling one province of its culture.

The French expression for the wider, rather than the narrow, approach to learning is *haute vulgarisation*. The word is easily misunderstood – it seems to have to do with 'vulgar'. But it means diffusion on a high (i.e. academic) level. This intention was both behind my teaching at the university and my writing while a professor. Most of the contributions I have published were book reviews and articles on Japanology in either English, German or French. The greater part of my writing in these forty years was done in Japanese. Little of it was done for highly specialized journals of interest only to scholars in the same field. Such contributions are necessary and I read them avidly myself. But I thought at the time, and still think, that a journal for university men in general would well represent the views of learning, humanism and intercultural relations characteristic of our small university, in the academic world of Japan.

Whether the quarterly has been a success or not, is not for me to say. Too much of my personal thinking and feeling went into every issue, and too many memories, overwhelmingly happy ones, are connected with each author and each article. But I do know that my experience has been that of many of my colleagues: to spread one's knowledge in one field to experts in another field is one of the happiest but also one of the hardest intellectual experiences. It is connected with the discovery of the power of the word. Additional energy is needed for an article on philosophy which a jurist or an engineer should also be able to follow.

This is doubly true when it comes to translating from a foreign language. Not only is, say, a German apt to consider his readers familiar with the principal works of Goethe. The translator, who may also be a specialist in German literature, may show his pride in his craft by writing a Japanese language as near as possible to German, hence unintelligible to the average reader. Many years ago I showed to a colleague a text of mine, which a friend had translated into Japanese. I thought it was a masterpiece because it flowed so easily. But my colleague stated: 'It doesn't have the feel of German. It's a bad translation. Too facile.' Fortunately, this kind of attitude is disappearing.

It would be wonderful to be able to say that we at our quarterly have contributed to the new trend of thinking of translation as a highly creative art in which the feel for Japanese matters as much as that for the original. At any rate, we have tried to follow such standards at a time when they were far less in evidence than they are now. People tell me that a new school of academic writing – or at least academic translating – has started from our quarterly. I know this is stark flattery; one cannot compare the almost alpine heights of academic publishing in Japan with the little hill of our quarterly. But I confess this flattery warms my heart a little. All the dreams of my childhood, the acquisition of languages, the contact with different cultures, the study at universities in various countries and my settled life in Japan had contributed to make me work for an international and interdisciplinary academic journal an intense pleasure.

My life as a university man (*daigakujin*) in Japan should have caused plenty of strain. Instead it turned out to be a source of ever renewed satisfaction. This is also true of my job in charge of the committee editing a scholarly magazine. The very fact that – in contrast to ordinary contributions – we solicited our manuscripts rather than waiting for them to be submitted, or again the fact that we would occasionally turn down contributions if they were not fit for the issue we had planned, or also submit hints for improvement – could easily hurt people's feelings. Did it help to be a foreigner not necessarily familiar with the *honne* (real intention or 'private face') behind the graciously displayed *tatemae* (for the sake of appearances, or 'public face')? Or were bad feelings occasionally created from sheer clumsiness? I do not know, and for the smooth running I have to thank my collaborators. During my thirty years of editing I came into far closer contact with Japanese intellectuals than many foreigners who live in Japan. But it was also true fulfilment of a dream, the dream of a bridge-builder.

So was the publication of books. From the office of the quarterly *Sophia* we arranged the publication of a number of monographs on French, German and English Literature, Marxist and Scholastic Philosophy and other books of the humanities. We also edited volumes of *Kyōdō Kenkyū* (joint research) on such themes as *Daigaku to Humanism*, (universities and humanism), *Dentō to Sōzō*, (tradition and imagination) *Gekidō suru Shakai to Daigaku* (society in turmoil and universities) etc.

The most successful of my compilations – at least to judge from the book reviews and letters received, and from the copies sold – was *Gendai Shichō* (modern thought) *to* (and)

Catholicism. It was a collection of articles, for which I succeeded in mobilizing twenty-five authors from Germany, France, England and the United States and an equal number of Japanese translators. On opening once more this volume of 500 pages my heart fills with nostalgia. Of the contributors who, twenty years ago, courteously sent in manuscripts or permitted reprints, quite a few are no longer alive; they all evoke in me signposts in my own spiritual development: Christopher Dawson, Gabriel Marcel, Romano Guardini, Hugo Rahner, Karl Adam, Martin D'Arcy, Bertrand Russell, Courtney Murray, François Mauriac and Evelyn Waugh. I wish now I had kept their personal letters in the original. Of the translators, Kobayashi Yoshio, Chikayama Kinji and Fukase Motohiro have also died. And the other contributors and translators alike are of my own generation, now perhaps busy reminiscing as I am. I think we all did our jobs for mental comprehension of the post-war *bundan* (world of letters). We probably also think that our activity then was hard work. Yet it must be confessed, that such books could more easily be written two decades ago. The break with our own past was not as drastic as it seems to be becoming at present. The electronic computer and connected inventions of the Second Industrial Revolution had not yet created the vital problems to which no answers are yet known. Much of the self-assurance has disappeared from public argument these days, and that is a good thing. I was proud in those days when, judging from these essays, I learned that Catholicism was not really so exclusive as is often thought, and it is true that I went to great efforts to secure wherever possible liberal views on Catholic Christianity. The book was intended as a contribution to comparative culture. It was not to be apologetic nor polemical.

But while after twenty years we have become less polemical, we have also become more flabby. As a priest and educator I continually come across both parents and their offspring, lamenting the old days with their certainties. But that is a problem no longer of one culture as against another, but of a revolution quickly going on in the modern world behind the façade of cultural differences.

Reminiscing about the heroic times of editing *Gendai Shichō to Catholicism,* I cannot but think of the many Japanese friends of those days supporting and encouraging me. The writer's and editor's job can be lonely. There is no reaction to the written word as there is, even among the shy and reticent Japanese, to the spoken word. But I was fortunate in having caring friends, of whom I mention here only a very few of those no longer around. Tanaka Kōtarō, whom I have known longest, looked on me with that affection which the Japanese *sensei* reserves for a favourite disciple and I needed this affection struggling as I was in unknown territory. I compare him with another Tanaka Tadao, formerly of Ehime *Shōka Daigaku* (University of Commerce) and later founder and long-time principal of Aikō *Gakuen* (college). When studying as a young *kōshi* (lecturer) in Germany, he had been living in my parents' house; now he adopted me almost as if I were his younger brother. Inviting me for a few days stay with him in Matsuyama in 1936, one year after my first arrival, he spoke to me only in Japanese, although he was fluent in German, and my Japanese was still poor. Nothing in all these nearly fifty years has given me greater confidence.

Abe Nōsei, like Tanaka Kōtarō also a *Mombu Daijin* (Minister of Education) for a while, represented to me the spirit of that peculiarly Japanese humanism, a humanism of Meiji years, which was so vital in the reconstruction period after the war. Once I was standing behind him in a reception by NHK to welcome a German tenor. As the tune of *Lindenbaum* filled the room, the big man's shoulders shook with silent sobbing.

My own tears almost came, as I thought of the faithfulness to both his own and the European culture in a period of violent changes. Amano Teiyū, like Abe was a trusted adviser to me for years and he could graciously pronounce, in his serious way, a word of appreciation for something I had written or said. A pat on the shoulder from such a sage was an unexpected pleasure. It seemed in itself to justify the labour of learning the Japanese language and continued studying of its culture. 'You really seem to like the Japanese', Kawabata Yasunari (1899–1972) once said to me, apparently after reading something by me. We met occasionally, not only at Pen Club meetings, but also on the near Sanada-bori when he stayed in *Fukudaya* (inn), near my university. He was a shy, sensitive man, and to this day I believe – as do a few other people – that he did not commit suicide but died in an accident. (Incidentally, nor do I think that Mishima Yukio[55] envied him his Nobel Prize.) He liked Mishima, and when I told him that I found some of Mishima's novels difficult reading, he told me not to bother looking up every unknown *kanji* in the dictionary, but leave it for its decorative purpose and not worry about the meaning. As for Mishima, I have never known a more courteous Japanese. At the same time I have never known one more *energisch*; he was the incarnation, as I have written in some *tsuitō bun* (memorial book), of Schopenhauer's *Die Welt als Wille und Vorstellung* (The World as Will and Fantasy (Imagination)).' The power of his will and fantasy were almost un-Japanese.

I have to leave out of this account a great many fields of work for inter-cultural understanding, such as symposia, radio and television talks, lecture tours through the country, articles for the press.

Brief mention should be made, however, of my activity as visiting professor abroad. My first such work was for Fordham University in New York where I was invited in 1956 for a course in the Summer School. I lectured over a six-week period on Japanese Cultural History, very much as I had been doing in the International Division in Tokyo. The audience consisted of some thirty young men and women, mostly interested in teaching jobs in Japan. I found them to be refreshingly frank and uninhibited. At the same time I discovered very little problem consciousness. These were the times before Vietnam and Iran, and the American way of life was still believed in as the best without a shadow of doubt. Still, much as Americans are now the leading scholars of Japan, so in this little class I ran into a few remarkably talented young men who, upon direct contact with Japan later on, blossomed into veritable experts of comparative culture. This was my first visit to the United States. I was much older than I had been when crossing first the frontiers from Germany to other European countries and from Europe to Japan. I did not experience, therefore, any kind of cultural shock, but, equally, I did not learn as much as I had from other countries.

My second teaching experience came a year or two later when Ryūkyū University invited me to lecture for a few weeks on 'English literature seen against its European background'. The few weeks in Okinawa brought me, in contrast to New York, near to a cultural shock. I realized for the first time how immensely the people had suffered during the war. I also heard from Okinawan friends of the cultural neglect and disrespect they had suffered at the hands of Japanese military men and administrators. I made friends with quite a few students who taught me a number of phrases in a dialect near Muromachi (fifteenth century) Japanese. My enthusiastic account for *Kokoro* was later reprinted in a book *Waga Okinawa* (Our Okinawa) of several tomes.

The National Universities both of Australia (Canberra) and New Zealand (Auckland) have invited me to teach in their Asian Departments. When thinking of the contempt in which both countries used to hold the 'yellow races', their switch to serious study of Japan must be called remarkable. My impression of Australia was more, that of New Zealand less, favourable than I had expected. The Australians are not at all as provincial and materialistic as I have heard them described, and the New Zealanders are economically so weak that little of their famous free-and-easy spirit remains alive in the present climate of cultural despondency. As I was lecturing on Japan – with the help of Japanese texts – to these eager learners, I was often wondering: would some of the present intellectual curiosity have prevented the Pacific War? If the Japanese had been better known – instead of being seen through the prejudiced eyes of white jingoists – they might have been allowed to immigrate, aggression against China might have been prevented, and Australia and New Zealand would be better off too.

In Europe I have never been a proper visiting professor but I have lectured in Tübingen, Innsbruck, Louvain and Oxford. The general academic atmosphere both in German-speaking and in French-speaking countries is very much to my heart. The jolly, joking tone matters less than in America and Australia, and the over-refined tone of speaking and writing as in Oxford is unknown. Indeed, general knowledge about Asia is declining in the European countries, the more English becomes the world language. Native scholars of Eastern cultures decrease. As for England, it may for all intents and purposes have lost the war, it may be poor and its prospects may be dark, but it has retained some of the gifts that once made it great. These also include that empathy which is the presupposition of the comparative study of culture.

An Englishman who possessed this empathy with regard to Japan was Profesor Richard Storry[57] who invited me to St Anthony's, his College in Oxford, to lecture. It was an unforgettable experience to me. He died a short time ago and so I can call him by name as a great benefactor in my field of studies. I like him not only because of his valuable books about Japanese history, but especially because of the spirit in which he studied an alien civilization, a spirit of simplicity and lucidity. This man of wide and deep learning said of himself when he came to Japan to receive an award from The Japan Foundation: 'At bottom I am a journalist manqué.' There is here the spirit both of humility and humour. So learned a man was not a mere journalist, since he knew too much. But he was not 'manqué either, because while a scholar he could write lucidly and even thrillingly. He was a real comparatist.

Writing the autobiography of my *kenkyū* (research, studies) I cannot really report on a peculiar scientific method; I cannot even propose an original definition of my field, be it comparative literature or comparative culture, and I definitely cannot recount any startling discoveries. I have only reported how, from early on, circumstances of place and time brought me into the vicinity of several cultural climates in Europe, how lucky I was to profit from this accident and how fortunate I was to be able to delve into these cultures at the university, and for the rest of my life teach and write about my early experiences, again at the university and, again, in another culture which was almost to become my own. I have always cared for other cultures and literatures with exuberance and out of love. Numerous colleagues and disciples, readers and friends have told me that to look at the world by way of comparison is indeed exhilaratingly satisfactory. Never has the world been so pluralistic and so easily accessible.

The life-long study of several cultures and, even more, the life of a man from one culture, never abandoned, spent in another culture chosen as his final home. And, one would imagine, the strain must be heightened if the man is a priest. Of me I can confess that the opposite is the case. I never felt constricted by the otherness of my surroundings, from the day in my youth when I first crossed the border to live for a while with the French. To me as a priest the secular civilization outside my religious house is, in a sense, also alien country. But the two modes of life have not produced tension but stimulation. I have never felt shut out from modern society because I lived the life of a celibate, sacrificing part of his independence by leading a community life without private income.

I do not want to enter here into the question whether priestly celibacy is a good thing or not. Let it only be noted that it has played a large and rather beneficial role not only in

Catholicism, but in other higher religions such as Hinduism, Buddhism both of the Small and Large Vehicles, not to mention several religions of antiquity. The celibate life for reasons of idealism is definitely not a simple matter for a healthy adult. And it is certainly harder in our present world than it was even when I was young. The internal combustion engine, electronics and the computer have helped spread the hedonist mentality. The idea of lasting values transcending the pleasure of the moment appears threatened by a great many modern ways of life. The indulgence of the flesh matters rather than its mortification. Maybe things will reach the point in our advanced society where an unmarried clergy may die out. It would be regretable. The priesthood has brought happiness to many, both those who sincerely embraced the faith of the priest and those who profited from its service. Meanwhile, the increasing secularization of industrialized society is reaching its full course. The pendulum may swing back.

The pendulum may swing back, in other words, the extremes of hedonism, secularism and consumerism may lead to the search for more lasting and more rewarding values. Some time ago, on a visit to Europe, I had a number of conversations along those lines with people of very different backgrounds.

With my brother's family I spent several days along the beaches of the Adriatic near Venice, where Germans assemble each summer by the hundreds of thousands. As we were sitting in the shade by the quiet, deep-blue sea, with the younger generation energetically busy building muscles or acquiring a tan, one of my conversation partners said: 'I, too, have an uncle, a priest.'

'But no son or nephew, I surmise.

'No, aren't priests dying out?'

'No, no, no.' Quite a tempestuous chorus of disagreeing voices broke out. Especially the younger members of our group were sure that a balance in evaluation was about to be restored. Teenagers, I was told, want to return to nature, to purity, to clear beliefs, to sacrifice. I am sure much of it was exaggerated. But when I later returned to my home in Germany, experts in such matters – theologians, sociologists and educators – confirmed the impression of that talk with German salarymen and artisans at the Lido seaside, namely, that the supernatural dimension was being rediscovered by the young.

A month later, I had a similar talk with French friends. I had been back to the locale of my studies, half a century ago, in the old city of Le Puy in Central France. We were sitting at an outdoor café in the Cathedral plaza on a late summer evening. My friends were a married couple of my age. But they had invited relatives and acquaintances of various generations to meet the guest from Japan. The talk turned to religion as the Angelus began to be rung from the cathedral and the church spires. 'Alas,' an elderly lady sighed, 'religion does not mean much any more to the French.' I mentioned my own reminiscences of the villages in this very vicinity fifty years earlier. How I had encountered, for the first time, a peasantry indifferent to religion, and reflected that this was probably due to the strongly atheistic prejudices of the French Revolution.

This remark became the signal for a talk as excited as that on the Lido. Some of the younger generation seemed to think that atheism was passé. It was boring. But to the question 'What, then, is coming?', there was no real answer. Salvation is expected, in France, from the cities, and I was told by several that the young in the cities were increasingly attracted to spiritual renewal, to meditation, social work, etc. 'Will there be more priests?' The answers were evasive – but not negative.

As for celibacy, the people here, too, were remarkably conservative. Far from unnatural, an unmarried priest seemed to them to inspire friendly affection, and also the kind of severity and seriousness needed in the modern world. That is what I said as we emptied our last Pernod while the darkness gathered over the market-place.

The fact remains – and this brings us back to the general

tenor of the present report – the duality of cultural experience can lead to deeper understanding and richer experience. Every day I had to face two worlds: one, our religious house with its regular hours of prayer, meals, conversation and study, among men of different nationalities (two languages are officially used on bulletin boards and public addresses, Japanese and English, but you may also use other languages wherever they are understood); two, the world outside, lecturing, writing, visiting friends, attending *gasshuku* (boarding house) or *gakkai* (academia), taking walks, travelling.

My principal fear while in Japan always was to be mistaken for a proselytizer. The word '*senkyōshi*' (missionary) has unpleasant connotations in Japanese. The persistence of *oshiuri* (aggressive selling) from door to door, or pointedly refraining from sake and tobacco, or disturbing a cheerful crowd of *hatsumōde*[58] (first visit to a shrine in the New Year) at *Kōbō Daishi*,[59] Kawasaki – these are exasperating examples of the 'missionary' spirit in its disliked form. Less conspicuous but equally contemptible is the attitude of the missionary who abuses his authority as a teacher to propagate his religious convictions. If I have never done this – as I hope I can say – I owe it to my entire upbringing, my family and my Order, not least my to my special *kenkyū* (research), the study of similarities and differences in cultures and literatures. I have learned to look at my own scheme of values with a certain detachment.

The question may arise: why should I, although no zealot, volunteer to be in Japan to preach my religious faith? In a simplified way the answer is similar to the motive of my teaching and writing about language and literature. As I want to share the joys of the languages and cultures of my field – from exuberance, one might almost say – so also was I willing to initiate interested Japanese into the profound, namely, religious background of my European heritage.

There is, of course, more to religion than the mere conveyance of facts and reasons. The need for religion we feel most acutely in what Jaspers calls *Grenzsituation* – the predicament where man feels confronted with existential problems, a cul-de-sac, a fate beyond his strength. From people in such plights have come the hundreds I had the joy to baptize. They had met me, or somebody else, while searching for a deeper purpose to life.

I should add here a word of explanation to the term *Grenzsituation*. A few years ago, the special correspondent of one of the most important German newspapers, the *Frankfurter Allgemeine*, came to ask me about the influence of religion in modern Japan. Like many foreign observers he held several mistaken ideas about Japanese religiosity as being profit-seeking (*goriyaku*), superficial, unconnected with morality, in short, not serious. Well, I think I can say that I changed some of these mistaken views. However, when I quoted the Japanese sensitiveness to *Grenzsituation*, I at first failed to make my point. He seemed to take the word as indicating a kind of *Kurushii toki no kami-danomi.* (turning to God at a time of trouble) 'I find this repulsive,' he said, 'to admit the need for god only when you find yourself in a cul-de-sac. It's like making God a means for man's needs – God is made subservient to man.' He was quite disgusted.

I think I succeeded in clarifying my friend's misunderstanding. Jaspers was, of course, not talking of religion as a quick remedy in an hour of need. *Grenzsituation* is precisely that point where man faces the darkness of total solitude and like lightning, the reality of another world, the supernatural world, becomes visible for a momentary flash. Instead of feeling so strong that he could make God subservient to his will, he becomes so weak that he can do away with all illusion of the power of self – *jiriki*. My friend understood, but I felt slightly disheartened. If such misunderstandings can arise between men of the same language, background, in short, culture, how much more so when common points are fewer. How much of what was evident to me must have been baffling to my Japanese interlocutors. Yet they were too polite to point it out.

My double function – priest and professor – has been to me a cause of happiness rather than discomfort. I can imagine that it must be harder for a priest specializing in econometrics or hydraulic engineering. But literature touches on values which also concern religious faith. I have never regretted being a priest, and as far as my life in Japan is concerned, my being a priest has helped me find more friends and probe deeper into Japan than my being a scholar.

The whole of my life I have lived between *samazama no* (a variety of) cultures, equally at home in all, but, I hope, never so smug and self-satisfied as to sit in judgement. It is for others to judge what I could have done better, and I am sure there is much more to criticize than to applaud. As for my debt to Japan, I have tried to sum it up in two recent books: *Nihon to Watakushi* (Japan and I) (Nansōsha) and *Wakon Yōkon* (Kōdan-sha). Since I arrived here, in 1935, the story of *Tōzai Bunka Kōryū* (East-West cultural interchange) has made revolutionary progress, although I believe that still more work has to be done on the deeper level of religious and moral understanding. The task is becoming more urgent, as the industrialized welfare states of both Japan and the West begin to show signs of moral weakness. Another world confrontation is becoming topical, not only cultural but also social and economic. This calamity is rapidly drawing near. The blueprints of engineers and politicians will, by the end of the century, become utterly insufficient to help decisively. They will need the heroism of the young who want to go out for reasons of unselfish idealism.

Many friends and enemies of Japan keep saying that the Japanese are neither fit nor willing to provide effective help to the people in the third world. The best argument I have against such people comes from my own family. One of my sisters (now dead) worked for many decades in Bombay, India, one in Punjab, Pakistan, one in Parana, Brazil. Without Japanese help, they would be unable to accomplish what they do: Japanese Sisters, volunteers, benefactors. The Japanese, no doubt, are shy, awkward in language, gesture, improvization, easily embarrassed by both blame and praise, failure and success. But if I can trust my sisters' verdict, nobody is more thoroughly trustworthy than the Japanese, nobody more sensitive to feelings of compassion and social justice, while also more practical and inventive.

I look forward to Japan becoming a country producing young volunteers to go abroad and help the less blessed, as Europe still did when I was young. It would be the most wonderful way of integrating *kenkyū* (study) with life.

Postscript

As I re-read these pages, I find the early part more interesting. No doubt, events recorded by the brain earlier stand out more clearly. My *sempai* (senior) and *dōryō* (colleagues), the late Fr von Küenburg, an Austrian Count, suffered aphasia from a brain stroke. He learned to speak again: first, the Viennese dialect, the language of his wet-nurse; second, high German, the language of his mother; third French, the language of his governess; fourth, English acquired later; last, but never fluently again, Japanese. So my youthful memories are vivid enough to flow through my pen.

But apart from brain cells, the impact of my family and school must have been decisive, especially in enlarging my mental horizons in the international and religious direction. Has, then, my path through life been set by inheritance and education? Of course not. Only as I continue with my narrative into later decades, the past slowly glides into the present. The tale becomes dull, since we think we already know what is happening.

Names Index

—————————— oOo ——————————